It was a special experience to read Dan⌐
noticed that something was happening⌐
the mystery of God's Word. All the d⌐
diamond of the Bible touched me, humbled me, and brought me
to worship the God of the Scriptures: what a privilege that God
speaks to us. What a miracle that He opens His heart to us. What
a recreating power we experience in God's speaking. What absolute
assurance overwhelms us through the witness of the Spirit in the
Word. What awesome depths of salvation open up before us. How
inexhaustible are these treasures. I praise the infallible Word and I
invite you to share in this experience.

WILLEM VAN VLASTUIN
Professor of Theology and Spirituality of Reformed Protestantism, Vrije
Universiteit Amsterdam

The substance of the Christian life is that in knowing God we know
ourselves. To put it differently, God's will is that in answering the
question, 'Who is Jesus Christ?,' we may truly answer the question,
'Who am I?' The only way to find an answer to those questions is
the meditative and contemplative reading of the Word of God with
the Church through the ages. Contrary to some misconceptions by
Roman Catholicism and Eastern Orthodoxy, Protestantism has a
living tradition on the skill of the meditative and contemplative
reading of Scripture. As the Puritan divine Thomas Manton wrote
in his ten sermons on Genesis 24:63, 'In these solitary and heavenly
retirements...we have most experience of God and of ourselves.'
This book by Danny Hyde helps us to know what the Word of God
is, where we can find it, and then how we can learn the art of the
spiritual reading of Scripture as the Word of God for our lives.

ANDREA FERRARI
Pastor of the *Chiesa Riformata di Perugia*, Italy

As Dr. Hyde rightly says at the beginning of this book, the difficult
days of the apostle Paul are no different from ours. The Word of God
continues to be doubted, denied, and destroyed. The curious thing
is that this even permeates the life of the church among professing
believers. For this reason I believe this book is pertinent for our
days. In simple words, Dr. Hyde approaches "bibliology" and puts
it into practice. He says something very interesting about applying

the doctrine of the Word: "'we are to read the Word as an act of spiritual warfare." This is what we need in our churches today—not nominal believers, but real believers who live by every Word that comes from the mouth of God.

Luis Alarico
Director del Programa Interno, Seminario Reformado Latinoamericano

I never cease to be amazed by the supernatural character of Christianity. The Bible we hold in our hands has been breathed-out by God himself! For that reason, Scripture is our final authority, trustworthy in every way, and sufficient for our salvation—yes, the Word of God is powerful indeed. With the compassion of a pastor, the fortitude of a theologian, and the wits of a historian, Daniel Hyde sets our footing on this sure foundation. Yet when he celebrates our Protestant heritage, he is wise to plant us in the soil of reformed catholicity. The Reformers were not innovators but their dependency on scripture was an ancient doctrine, the continual refrain of the one, holy, catholic, and apostolic church.

Matthew Barrett
Associate Professor of Christian Theology at Midwestern Baptist Theological Seminary and author of *The Reformation as Renewal and God's Word Alone*

# *This is the* WORD *of the* LORD

## Becoming Confident in the Scriptures

## Daniel R. Hyde

CHRISTIAN
FOCUS

Copyright © Daniel R. Hyde 2023

paperback ISBN 978-1-5271-0941-4
ebook ISBN 978-1-5271-0999-5

10 9 8 7 6 5 4 3 2 1

Published in 2022
by
Christian Focus Publications Ltd,
Geanies House, Fearn, Ross-shire,
IV20 1TW, Great Britain.

www.christianfocus.com

Cover design by Daniel Van Straaten

Printed and bound by
Bell & Bain, Glasgow

MIX
Paper | Supporting
responsible forestry
FSC
www.fsc.org FSC® C007785

# Contents

Foreword     9

Introduction     13

1   Finding God's Word in Our Time (2 Tim. 4:1-5)     19

2   Certainty: 'The Prophetic Word More Fully Confirmed'     27
    (2 Peter 1:16-21)

3   Revelation: 'He Has Spoken to Us' (Hebrews 1:1-2a)     35

4   Inspiration: 'Breathed Out by God' (2 Timothy 3:16)     45

5   Authority: 'Let Them Hear Them' (Luke 16:22-31)     53

6   Canonicity: 'The Law, the Prophets, and the Psalms'     65
    (Luke 24:44-45)

7   Sufficiency: 'Complete, Equipped for Every Good Work'     75
    (2 Timothy 3:14-17)

8   Perspicuity: 'Open My Eyes That I May Behold' (Psalm 119:18)     87

9   Reading the Word: 'He Shall Read It' (Deuteronomy 17:18-20)     99

10   Experiencing the Word: 'Reviving the Soul' (Psalm 19:7-11)     113

Appendix 1: John Chrysostom on Daily Bible Reading     123

Appendix 2: J.C. Ryle's 'Short Hints' on Bible Reading     131

Appendix 3: Prayer of John Chrysostom Before Reading or     135
Listening to the Word of God

*To those seeking and striving to build their houses of faith on the solid rock foundation of Jesus' words and not the shifting sands of human ideology and philosophy.*

*Blessed Lord,*
*who hast caused all holy Scriptures to be written for our learning:*
*Grant that we may in such wise*
*hear them,*
*read,*
*mark,*
*learn,*
*and inwardly digest them,*
*that by patience and comfort of thy holy Word,*
*we may embrace and ever hold fast the blessed hope of everlasting life,*
*which thou hast given us in our Saviour Jesus Christ.*
*Amen.*

The Second Sunday in Advent
*Book of Common Prayer (1662)*

# Foreword

Let us night and day muse and have meditation and contemplation in them; let us ruminate and, as it were, chew the cud, that we may have the sweet juice, spiritual effect, marrow, honey, kernel, taste, comfort and consolation of them.[1]

Archbishop Thomas Cranmer

We live in a time of unprecedented sophistication, restlessness, insecurity and rancor. The media and other influential voices have empowered their followers to view ancient texts and great books from the past with suspicion and irrelevance. The 'cancel culture' machine attempts to silence those who speak Truth into the midst of our day through ridicule and dismissive gongs, pushing to the margins those who believe in the old, old story of Jesus and His love for me.

Many Christians, churches and denominations appear to be having a crisis of confidence in the Word of God written. Today's 'woke' influencers, have decided that it is no longer viable to believe that ordinary men and women, inspired by the Holy Spirit, received the Word of God and wrote it down for their generation and those

---

1.    'A Fruitful Exhortation to the Reading and Knowledge of Holy Scripture,' in *The Books of Homilies: A Critical Edition*, ed. Gerald Bray (Cambridge: James Clarke & Co, 2015), 13.

who came after them to receive, believe and proclaim. The fact is, that over the last 100 years, there has been one wave after another of attack on the Bible—the inspiration, the inerrancy and the sufficiency of Scripture.

Throughout history, some Christians have always wanted something more than the Bible. They have sought traditions, charismatic experiences and decrees from church leaders to compliment the truth of the Bible—always wanting to add something extra as a result of their lack of confidence in the Word of God alone. When this happens, the Word of God becomes distorted; and Christ, who is revealed in the Gospels, becomes veiled. Continually searching for something more only serves to make us restless. In this book, author Danny Hyde quotes one of my own heroes, Anglican Bishop J.C. Ryle, who taught that when we keep searching and looking and wandering, we enter a pathless wilderness.[2]

How true this has been in my own denomination which left its former ecclesiastical moorings because of what started as a gentle drift away from the Bible and resulted in riding white water rapids towards inevitable division and destruction. When this happens with a Christian, or a congregation, or a denomination, a course correction is necessary. Our course correction came in 2008 when faithful Anglicans gathered in Jerusalem and unanimously agreed to the Jerusalem declaration which states that *we believe the Holy Scriptures of the Old and New Testaments to be the Word of God written and to contain all things necessary for salvation. The Bible is to be translated, read, preached, taught and obeyed in its plain and canonical sense, respectful of the church's historic and consensual reading.*[3]

Danny Hyde writes with certainty about these same truths in this book. He concludes that we have a sure refuge in the God who sufficiently revealed Himself in the Scriptures for what it means to be a Christian. He emphasizes a daily reading and contemplation of the Bible. He writes about the office of the preacher and the proclamation of the Word of God and he firmly confronts those churches that have made additions to the Bible while winsomely inviting the reader to a place of renewed confidence that the Bible is God's complete and final word to humanity.

---

2.  J.C. Ryle, *Expository Thoughts on the Gospels:* Luke 1–10, 4 volumes (Grand Rapids: Baker Book House, reprinted 2007), 2:371.

3.  See https://www.gafcon.org/about/jerusalem-declaration

How utterly amazing to consider that Almighty God, the creator of the universe, who parted the Red Sea, fed a multitude of people with five loaves and two fish and raised the crucified Messiah from the grave still speaks to us today through the Bible!

In the pages of this book, you will discover that the Bible is living and is endued with life. It is a living word and not a dead book. The words of the Old Testament prophets, the songs of the Psalms, the New Testament Gospels and Epistles are not dead letters upon a page, they are living words full of vibrant heart-piercing life. I like to think of the Bible as having hands to lay hold of you, feet to run after you, power to subdue you and to search out thoughts deep within your mind. As we embrace it, we are reformed by it.

This was the view of the English reformers of the sixteenth century, many of whom gave their lives in defense of the Word of God as articulated in Article VI of the *Thirty-Nine Articles of Religion*, which says, *Holy Scriptures containeth all things necessary to salvation: so that whatsoever is not read therein, nor may be proved thereby, is not to be required of any man, that it should be believed as an article of the faith, or be thought requisite or necessary to salvation.*

I am thankful to God that Danny has written this book. As you read it, pray that God the Holy Spirit would be your teacher and your guide. Pray that He would restore your confidence in the Bible as the Word of God written. Pray like the psalmist,

*Oh how I love your law!*
*It is my meditation all the day.*
*Your commandment makes me wiser than my enemies,*
*for it is ever with me.* (Ps. 119:97, 98)

The Rt. Rev. Julian M. Dobbs, Bishop
*Anglican Diocese of the Living Word*

# Introduction

'This is the Word of the Lord.' In my congregation and in congregations around the world, Christians hear this refrain every week after the Scriptures have been read. In response, we say, 'Thanks be to God!' Can you make this simple yet profound confession of faith? Can you sing with the hymn writer, 'Holy Bible, book *Divine*'?[1] Even more, do you have the confidence in these Scriptures to say, 'Precious treasure, thou art *mine*'? It's one thing to know that God's people have made this confession for millennia, yet another thing even to acknowledge that your church, denomination, and tradition of churches confesses this, but what's most important is that *you* have this confidence for yourself. That's why I'm writing this short book. I want you to become confident in the Word of God. I want you to know for certain that God speaks to you in and through the pages of the Bible.

The Lord warned His disobedient people in the southern kingdom of Judah, where David once lived and from which tribe the Messiah would come, that even they would be disciplined for their sins by being sent into exile to Babylon. Then, when it seemed all hope would be lost in that foreign land beyond the horizon, the Lord commanded the prophet Isaiah to proclaim that 'comfort' would arise once again. Besides His promise, what assurance did the Lord give that this comfort would be real? While 'the grass'

---

1. From the hymn, "Holy Bible, Book Divine" by John Burton (1803)

13

and 'the flower' of human ability and power 'withers' and 'fades,' the Lord proclaimed, 'but the word of our God will stand forever' (Isa. 40:8). Our confidence in God is rooted in the reality that He has spoken in it.

Yet, at the heart of why I'm writing this book is that as a pastor I know that we, as God's people, don't always have such assurance and confidence that the Bible we hold in our hands is what our forefathers called *ipsissima verba*, 'the very words themselves' from God.[2] Why not? Because although 'the law of the Spirit of life has set [us] free in Christ Jesus from the law of sin and death' (Rom. 8:2), and we 'walk…according to the Spirit' (Rom. 8:4), 'live according to the Spirit' and 'set [our] minds on the things of the Spirit' (Rom. 8:5), the sin nature we inherited from Father Adam still clings onto us like a body that is subject to death (Rom. 7:24; NIV 2011). One of the practical effects of our sin nature is that the fundamental doctrinal truth of the Bible as the Word of God, which we affirm in our heads, doesn't necessarily translate into experiential reality within our hearts. Theology doesn't always translate into biography.

Known as the greatest of the ancient Christian preachers, John

Chrysostom (347–407) once described this practical effect of the sin nature on his people's attitudes towards the Word. He reminded them in a sermon that 'I am ever urging, and shall not cease to urge, that you give attention, not only to the words spoken [in sermons], but that also, when at home in your house, you exercise yourselves constantly in reading the Divine Scriptures.'[3] He had to urge this because he lamented his people's response:

---

2. 'ipsissima verba.' Richard A. Muller, *Dictionary of Latin and Greek Theological Terms: Drawn Principally from Protestant Scholastic Theology* (Second edition, Grand Rapids: Baker Academic, 2017), 180.

3. 'ipsissima verba.' Richard A. Muller, *Dictionary of Latin and Greek Theological Terms: Drawn Principally from Protestant Scholastic Theology* (Second edition, Grand Rapids: Baker Academic, 2017), 60

> I am constantly busy in the courts...I am discharging public duties; I am engaged in some art or handiwork; I have a wife; I am bringing up my children; I have to manage a household; I am full of worldly business; it is not for me to read the Scriptures, but for those who have bid adieu to the world [i.e., monks].[4]

In contrast to the monks, he told his people, 'It is thy duty [to read the Scriptures] even more than theirs.'[5] Why would he say something that must have sounded so drastic to ancient ears? We 'are tossed in the midst of the sea, cannot avoid many failings, we ever stand in need of the immediate and constant comfort of the Scriptures.'[6] While monks

> rest far from the strife, and, therefore, escape many wounds... you stand perpetually in the array of battle, and constantly are liable to be wounded: on this account, you have more need of the healing remedies...there are surrounding us on all sides many causes and occasions of anger, many of anxiety, many of dejection or grief, many of vanity or pride; from all quarters, weapons are pointed at us. Therefore it is that there is need continually of the whole armour of the Scriptures.[7]

No doubt the people of Constantinople, whose preacher was the great Bishop Chrysostom, could say with their lips, 'This is the Word of the Lord.' Yet Chrysostom knew that their hearts had many practical struggles with this. What has brought this practical struggle home to me in a personal way as a Christian, as well as in my role as a pastor of people, is seeing some who professed such strong faith later renounce that faith *because they lost confidence in the Word.* Several years ago, this happened in such a way that stirred my passions to proclaim to my church family a doctrinal series on the Holy Scriptures of the Old and New Testaments being the Word of God. In quick succession a fellow pastor in my classis (region of churches) of my denomination (United Reformed Churches in North America) left for Eastern Orthodoxy. Then a

---

4. *Four Discourses of Chrysostom*, 60, 61.
5. *Four Discourses of Chrysostom*, 61.
6. *Four Discourses of Chrysostom*, 61.
7. *Four Discourses of Chrysostom*, 61, 62.

local Westminster Seminary California student converted to Roman Catholicism. Finally, a well-known Presbyterian Church in America pastor whom I know, and whose popular blog parishioners of mine read, announced that he no longer believed the Protestant doctrine of Scripture but now believed the claims of authority made by the Roman Church.[8]

We can so easily take it for granted for ourselves and in our churches that the Bible is the Word of God. We say that 'the Bible is God's Word' and that we belong to 'Bible-believing churches,' but do we know why? I believe Scripture evidences that every generation of God's people needs to appropriate for itself the truth of the Word of God as foundational and fundamental for saving faith. As the Heidelberg Catechism (1563) says, 'true faith' includes 'not only a sure knowledge by which I hold as true all that God has revealed to us in his Word' (Q&A 21). If we don't recommit ourselves to the Scriptures, I believe Scripture teaches that we will see a rapid shift from this generation into another 'that did not know the LORD' (Judg. 2:10). Paul exhorted Timothy, 'devote yourself to the public reading of Scripture, to exhortation, to teaching' (1 Tim. 4:13), precisely because 'in later times some will depart from the faith by devoting themselves to deceitful spirits and teachings of demons' (1 Tim. 4:1). He again told Timothy through his famous exhortation to 'preach the word' because 'the time is coming when people will not endure sound teaching' (2 Tim. 4:3).

There are challenges to the Scriptures being the Word of God in our lives every day, from every side, whether from a neighbor, on social media, or from television shows seeking to disprove the Word of God. In particular, there are claims from Roman Catholic and Eastern Orthodox theologians, co-workers, classmates, converts, and friends that we, as Protestants, need to answer confidently. We need to take the challenges of Roman Catholic and Orthodox family and friends seriously. We need to listen to their reasons for rejecting our doctrine of Scripture as being the place where God speaks certainly and sufficiently (*sola Scriptura*). Doing this, I believe, will lead us to recommit ourselves to 'hold[ing] as true all that God has revealed to us in his Word' (Heidelberg Catechism, Q&A 21). Such commitment will lead us to grow more and more

---

8. http://www.creedcodecult.com/a-heartfelt-farewell-to-the-presbyterian-church-in-america/ (Accessed December 23, 2020).

confident that, while grass and flowers whither and fade, 'the word of our God will stand forever' (Isa. 40:8). Thus, when the Scriptures are read aloud in public worship, and the reader says, 'This is the Word of the Lord,' I pray you can wholeheartedly say, 'Thanks be to God!' I pray you say this not just in that Sunday moment, but every day of your earthly pilgrimage until you enter eternal rest.

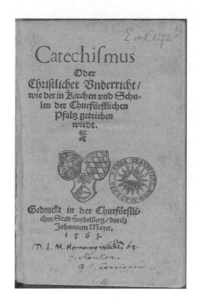

# Chapter 1

## *Finding God's Word in Our Time*

I charge you in the presence of God and of Christ Jesus,
who is to judge the living and the dead, and by his appearing
and his kingdom: preach the word; be ready in season and
out of season; reprove, rebuke, and exhort, with complete
patience and teaching. For the time is coming when people
will not endure sound teaching, but having itching ears they
will accumulate for themselves teachers to suit their own
passions, and will turn away from listening to the truth
and wander off into myths. As for you, always be sober-
minded, endure suffering, do the work of an evangelist,
fulfill your ministry (2 Tim. 4:1-5).

Statistics can be misleading if abstracted from the moment
they're calculated. In that moment, though, they reveal a glimpse of
reality. Ligonier Ministries' 2020 'The State of Theology' gives a sad
glimpse of the reality of contemporary American 'evangelicalism.'[1]
While 100 per cent of evangelicals strongly agreed with the
statement, 'The Bible is the highest authority for what I believe,'
many of them also said:

---

1.  http://thestateoftheology.com. On defining "evangelical/evangelicalism,"
see George M. Marsden, *Understanding Fundamentalism and Evangelicalism* (Grand
Rapids: Wm. B. Eerdmans Publishing Co., 1990) and Douglas A. Sweeney, *The
American Evangelical Story: A History of the Movement* (Grand Rapids: Baker, 2005).

- *'God accepts the worship of all religions, including Christianity, Judaism, and Islam.'* 42 per cent of evangelicals strongly or somewhat agree.
- *'The Holy Spirit can tell me to do something which is forbidden in the Bible.'* 18 per cent of evangelicals strongly or somewhat agree.
- *'The Bible, like all sacred writings, contains helpful accounts of ancient myths but is not literally true.'* 15 per cent of evangelicals strongly or somewhat agree.
- *'The Bible is 100 per cent accurate in all that it teaches.'* 9 per cent strongly or somewhat disagree or not sure.
- *'Religious belief is a matter of personal opinion; it is not about objective truth.'* 23 per cent strongly or somewhat agree.

These statistics go hand-in-hand with the sad reality that we see around us every day in which our culture in general, as well as professing Christians, is turning from the Word of God to alternative spiritualities, different religions, to themselves, or to no religion at all (the so-called 'Nones') for their version of the truth. Because of all this, the allure of Roman Catholicism and Eastern Orthodoxy fills a need for many evangelicals. Both promise the certainty of being *the* church in a sea of strip-mall churches. Both promise the comfort of unbroken succession back to the apostles in contrast to untrained pastors who just showed up in town. Both promise their tradition is authentic – Rome with its doctrine of Scripture and tradition being equally authoritative and Orthodoxy's Tradition being the work of the Holy Spirit in the Church, including Scripture.

*Finding God's Word in Our Time* is vital. It's my confident assertion that you and I can find God's Word in the Holy Scriptures, also known as the Bible. The thirty-nine books of the Old Testament and the twenty-seven of the New are where the authentic and living words of God to humanity are found.

## The Need to Find God's Word
There is an urgent need to find the authentic Word of God. The need of our time is no different than it was in times gone by. In his second epistle to young Pastor Timothy, Paul gives several characteristics of the 'last days' (2 Tim. 3:1). According to the New Testament – and not modern American 'prophecy experts' – it has been the 'last days' since our Lord's ministry on earth, from the time of His incarnation

(Heb. 1:1-2), crucifixion (Heb. 9:26), and effusion of His Spirit upon the apostles (Acts 2:1-4, 17).

The first characteristic of the last days is that the Church exists in an age of apostasy from the true faith. Paul says that 'people will not endure sound teaching, but having itching ears they will accumulate for themselves teachers to suit their own passions, and will turn away from listening to the truth and wander off into myths' (2 Tim. 4:3-4). This was true in the first century and still is true in the twenty-first. For example, in Paul's day some preached out of selfish ambition (Phil. 1:17) as well as for power and prestige (Acts 8:9-24). Today people desire fame and fortune, power and position, so they flock to 'name it and claim it,' 'word of faith,' and 'prosperity' preachers.

The second characteristic of the last days is that the Church exists in an age of ungodliness: 'people will be lovers of self, lovers of money, proud, arrogant, abusive, disobedient to their parents, ungrateful, unholy, heartless, unappeasable, slanderous, without self-control, brutal, not loving good, treacherous, reckless, swollen with conceit, lovers of pleasure rather than lovers of God, having the appearance of godliness, but denying its power' (2 Tim. 3:2-5). Again, as it was then, so it is now. For example, today so much of American Fundamentalism gives an appearance outwardly of godliness but lacks real Holy Spirit power. Don't drink, don't smoke, don't dance, don't wear short skirts (women), and don't grow your hair too long (men), is false piety.

Now, stop and ask yourself this question: what is so different about Paul's day and ours? The answer is absolutely nothing. Whether you're talking about the 50s, as in the first century, the 1550s, or the American good 'ole days' of the 1950s, the Church has always struggled to find the Word of God in its time. This is why in our age it's imperative that we find God's words to us and to the world. His words are like a beacon in the darkness of falsehood and like a light that exposes the darkness of our sinful hearts. When we find them, we find an anchor for our souls in the midst of the turbulent storms of false theology and false piety that beat against our faith. When we find them, we can speak them to the world calling it 'out of darkness into [the Lord's] marvelous light' (1 Peter 2:9).

## The Place to Find God's Word

So where can we find the true Word of God in our time? The Bishop of Rome says in Scripture and tradition, which ultimately means the Pope as arbiter of all truth, while Orthodoxy says in its living Tradition. It's interesting, isn't it, that in Paul's last letter that we know of, he 'charges' very seriously – on the basis of God's own presence and of Jesus' coming again as Judge – his spiritual son Timothy to 'preach *the word*' (2 Tim. 4:2). He calls that word 'sound teaching' (2 Tim. 4:3) and 'the truth' (2 Tim. 4:4). Preaching the Word was the purpose of Timothy's ministry (2 Tim. 4:5). In contrast to the word, the truth, and sound teaching, 'the time is coming when people' will turn instead to 'myths' (2 Tim. 4:4). From my vantage point, such myths would include those of Rome and Orthodoxy. Over time their mythology has grown into what it is today with the assertion and promise of certainty that they've never changed (unlike the thousands of Protestant churches) and that they have the only authentic interpretation of the truth of Scripture (unlike the uncertain and contradictory interpretations of thousands of Protestant churches).

In theological terms, the place to find God's Word is in the 'canon' of Scripture.[2] A canon (κανών, kanon) was an ancient way of describing what we call a ruler. Our ancient forefathers adapted this word for describing the Word of God, saying that we have in the Old and New Testaments the ruler, the true measure of authentic faith in God and genuine life before His face. In 2 Timothy 3 we learn of Timothy's upbringing in the faith of the Old Testament. Yet Paul's statement that 'all Scripture is breathed out by God' extends to the New Testament, of which Peter equates Paul's letters (2 Pet. 3:16) and which our Lord Himself says has come to an end with the Revelation of John (Rev. 22:18). In this collection, God 'makes himself known to us more openly by his holy and divine Word' (Belgic Confession, art. 2), that is, in

---

2. On the canon, see chapter 6 below.

the inspired, infallible, and canonical Scriptures of the thirty-nine books of the Old Testament and the twenty-seven of the New Testament. One important aspect of our Orthodox friends' belief is the personal presence of God through the means of Scripture. One Orthodox criticism of our Protestant view of Scripture is that we so focus on the Bible as text, as printed words, that we miss the Word who speaks in and through these words. It's not that our historic Protestant forefathers denied this, but that we may have buried it under the rubble from our modern 'battle for the Bible.' This criticism will come up again throughout this book, but for now, the language of the Belgic Confession (1561) addresses it simply: God 'makes himself known to us more openly by his holy and divine Word.' We, too, confess that the Word is the medium of God's own presence and voice today.[3]

The Scriptures of the Old and New Testaments are canonical because they are inspired, literally, 'God breathed' (2 Tim. 3:16).[4] As Peter says, the breath of God carried along the writers of Scripture like a sailboat upon the water (2 Pet. 1:20-21). These Scriptures are also sufficient. They are what we need to be 'complete' and 'equipped for every good work' (2 Tim. 3:17).[5]

## The Practice of Finding

But this is all assertion. How can you and I practically know that this is where God speaks? There are so many religious holy books out there, after all. Rome and Orthodoxy have powerful arguments we need to hear and thoughtfully respond to. Before he became the Bishop of Hippo (modern day Annaba, Algeria), Augustine (354–430) related his own story of practically searching for and finding God's Word. He began an investigation of Scripture, but as a pagan rhetorician, he did so with clever techniques. He said of this method: 'I was shutting the door of my Lord against myself by my misplaced attitude. I should have been knocking at it for it to be opened, but instead I was adding my weight to keep it shut.

---

3. On this, see Andrew Louth, *Introducing Eastern Orthodox Theology* (Downers Grove: InterVarsity Press, 2013), 8-10; Vladimir Lossky, *Orthodox Theology: An Introduction,* trans. Ian and Ihita Kesarcodi-Watson (Crestwood, NY: St. Vladimir's Seminary Press, 1978), 23-25.

4. On inspiration, see chapter 4 below.

5. On sufficiency, see chapter 7 below.

I was presuming to seek in my pride what can only be found by humility.'[6] Let us humbly read the Scriptures to hear the Lord of the Scriptures; let us search them to find *Him*.

The Westminster Confession of Faith (ch. I.5; 1646) gives us, as humble seekers, several reasons by which we can know that the Scriptures we read and search are the very words of God.[7] I'll summarize them here:[8]

First, they are majestic and pure, as we would expect from the mouth of God. One reading of the Bible next to the Apocrypha, the *Book of Mormon*, or the *Qu'ran* will evidence this.

Second, all the different parts of the Bible from Genesis to Revelation have a unity and consent; they all have the same scope or purpose in all the different genres of narrative, laws, poetry, prophecy, and letters, and although written over a vast expanse of 1,600 years, on different continents, and in different languages, they have a consent in these various parts as well as a unity of purpose, 'which is to give all glory to God' (Westminster Larger Catechism, Q&A 4; 1647).[9]

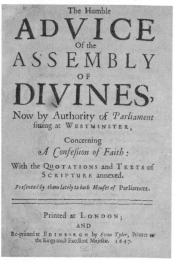

---

6. *Sermons 51–94*, trans. Edmund Hill, The Works of Saint Augustine: A Translation for the 21st Century, Volume 3 (Brooklyn: New City Press, 1991), 24. See also Augustine, *Confessions* 3.5 in *Confessions: Books 1–8*, trans. Carolyn J.-B. Hammond, Loeb Classical Library (Cambridge, MA: Harvard University Press, 2014), 105.

7. *Reformed Confessions of the 16th and 17th Centuries in English Translation: Volume 4, 1600–1693*, ed. James T. Dennison, Jr. (Grand Rapids: Reformation Heritage Books, 2014), 235.

8. I'll explain these in more detail in chapter 5.

9. *Reformed Confessions: Volume 4*, 300.

Third, they give light and are powerful to convert sinners and to comfort and build up believers unto salvation.

Fourth, the same Spirit who breathed them out also bears witness by and with them in our hearts (cf. Rom. 8:23-27). He alone is able fully to persuade us that these books are the very Word of God.

Knowing we've found God's Word in the canonical books of our Bibles, we need to practice the Word. We continually need to mine it for its riches by meditating on it (Ps. 1:1-2; Col. 3:16). This is a lifelong task, since, as Chrysostom said, 'It is not possible... ever to exhaust the mind of the Scriptures. It is a well which has no bottom.'[10] We continually need to seek to conform our lives to it (Ps. 119:1-8). We continually need to express our utter thankfulness for it (Ps. 119:62, 164). We continually need to be equipped to contend for it (Jude 3) by preserving it as well as by proclaiming it. May God help us to do so for our souls' sake, for the sake of our children, and for the sake of our churches.

## Conclusion

As yearly surveys and our own experience shows, we are living in a time of famine of the true Word of God. The ancient prophet Amos spoke of such a coming famine in his day: 'Behold, the days are coming, declares the Lord GOD, when I will send a famine on the land—not a famine of bread, nor a thirst for water, but of hearing the words of the LORD' (Amos 8:11). How true is this *still*? We are living in that day. This is why when we find the Word, we need to mine it for its riches, cultivate it for its food, and drink from it like a well in the desert. Sadly, Amos says in those days that 'they shall wander from sea to sea, and from north to east; they shall run to and fro, to seek the word of the LORD, but they shall not find it' (Amos 8:12). This describes our time. The apostate church blindly wanders from the sentimentality of Protestant Liberalism to the so-called authoritative and immovable word of Rome or Orthodoxy, to the relativistic Emerging Church, to the skeptical Bart Ehrman, to the happy Joel Osteen, and the list goes on. There is a lot of searching but no finding. Yet in the Word written, our searching turns to resting as the silence of our hearts is filled with His living voice.

---

10. Chrysostom, 'Homily 19 on Acts,' in *Nicene and Post-Nicene Fathers: First Series*, ed. Philip Schaff, 14 vols. (1889; repr., Peabody, MA: Hendrickson Publishers, fourth printing 2004), 11:127 col. 2.

# Chapter 2   CERTAINTY

## *The Prophetic Word More Fully Confirmed*

For we did not follow cleverly devised myths when we made known to you the power and coming of our Lord Jesus Christ, but we were eyewitnesses of his majesty. For when he received honor and glory from God the Father, and the voice was borne to him by the Majestic Glory, 'This is my beloved Son, with whom I am well pleased,' we ourselves heard this very voice borne from heaven, for we were with him on the holy mountain. And we have the prophetic word more fully confirmed, to which you will do well to pay attention as to a lamp shining in a dark place, until the day dawns and the morning star rises in your hearts, knowing this first of all, that no prophecy of Scripture comes from someone's own interpretation. For no prophecy was ever produced by the will of man, but men spoke from God as they were carried along by the Holy Spirit (2 Pet. 1:16-21).

If you've ever sprained an ankle, you know the feeling of uncertainty the first time you try to walk again. If you've ever studied for a test only to have questions you were unsure of, you know the feeling of uncertainty. If you've ever walked across an old, wobbly bridge, you know the feeling of uncertainty. There are many uncertainties in life. How much more do we need to be certain when it comes to the foundation of our faith and life as Christians? Our glorious and gracious Triune God is everything to us. Yet how do we know what we believe He's spoken to us is true? The Orthodox theologian, St. Theodore the Studite (759–826), paralleled the written Scriptures to icons (two-dimensional images), saying, 'What on the one hand is represented by ink and paper is represented on the other hand in the icon, thanks to the various colors and other materials.'[1] To paraphrase, the Scriptures are icons in ink. In other words, the Bible isn't the truth itself but the window to the Truth in Christ.[2] The beautiful face of our Lord is revealed and His living voice is heard as we open our Bibles and listen to it read and proclaimed publicly. But again, how do we know it is a true icon? That's why I'm writing. I want you to come to certainty about the Scriptures of our Old and New Testaments being the Word of God and therefore authoritative for doctrine and living. In this chapter, I want to look at 2 Peter 1 where we learn *the most certain thing we have in this life is the Word of God.*

Look at the whole of chapter 1 to establish that Peter is dealing with the issue of the certainty of the Word of God. He opens by saying that God's power has granted to us all we need for life and godliness through the knowledge of Christ, who calls us to His own glory and excellence (v. 3). By this glory and excellence He grants to us His precious and very great promises (v. 4). Through these promises we become partakers of God's divine nature (v. 4), which means becoming partakers of His holiness.[3] We experience this now in our conversion and sanctification (in contrast to our

1. Theodore Studite, *Antirrheticus*, 1, 10, in: PG 99, 339D, cited in Pope John Paul II's apostolic letter *Duodecimum Saeculum: On the Occasion of the 1200th Anniversary of the Second Council of Nicaea*, December 4, 1987, as found at http://www.vatican.va/content/john-paul-ii/en/apost_letters/1987/documents/hf_jp-ii_apl_19871204_duodecim-saeculum.html (Accessed January 7, 2021).

2. See Vladimir Berzonsky, 'Are Eastern Orthodoxy and Evangelicalism Compatible? No: An Orthodox Perspective,' in *Three Views on Eastern Orthodoxy and Evangelicalism*, eds. Stanley N. Gundry and Jasmes Stamoolis (Grand Rapids: Zondervan, 2004), 174-76; Louth, *Introducing Eastern Orthodox Theology*, 8-10.

3. See the succinct exegesis of Thomas Schreiner, *1, 2 Peter, Jude*, The New American Commentary 37 (Nashville: Broadman & Holman Publishers, 2003), 293-96. Al Wolters argues 'partakers of the divine nature' is idiomatic for fellowship with God in the covenant. '"Partners of the Deity": A Covenantal Reading of 2 Peter 1:4,' *Calvin Theological Journal* 25:1 (April 1990): 28-44. Richard Bauckham argues this 'sharing' is eschatological, meaning it will be experienced at the coming of Christ. 'Review of James M. Starr, *Sharers in Divine Nature: 2 Peter 1:4 in its Hellenistic Context.*' *The Journal of Theological Studies* 53:1 (April 2002): 278-81.

former corruption mentioned in verse 4) and we will experience it in its fullness in our glorification in the life to come. We see this as he goes on to say that we have escaped from the corruption of the world (v. 4). This is why he exhorts us to godly virtues in verses 5-9, saying if we do not grow in them, we have forgotten that we were cleansed from our former sins (v. 9). This is why we must make our calling and election sure (vv. 10-11). So in verses 12-15 Peter writes all this to give his readers the assurance that they have received the truth, especially as his time on earth draws to a close. In verses 3-15, Peter says the reason he's writing this letter is to teach us that we have been established in the truth of God's 'precious and very great promises' (2 Pet. 1:4); and having been established, he wants us to be certain of God's promised truth (vv. 16-21).

## The Certainty of Peter's Eye Witness

Peter builds his argument, first, with the certainty of his eye witness: 'For we did not follow cleverly devised myths when we made known to you the power and coming of our Lord Jesus Christ, but we were eyewitnesses of his majesty' (v. 16). The certainty that Peter offers is the certainty of one who lived with Jesus for three years. The Gospels record that Jesus chose and called him (Matt. 4:18-19). Then Peter walked with Him (Matt. 4:20). He ate with Him (Mark 2:15). He heard Jesus' teaching as one with authority (Matt. 7:28-29). He witnessed Jesus' astonishing signs and wonders (Matt. 8:1-17). He was there when Jesus was betrayed (Mark 14:43-46). Sadly, he was there denying the Lord when He was on trial (Mark 14:43-46). He saw the Lord risen from the dead (1 Cor. 15). He saw the wounds in His hands, feet, and side (John 20:26-29). He ate with the Lord after the resurrection (John 21:12-13) and was taught by Him for forty days before the Ascension (Acts 1:3). Peter, in particular, points out that he was there on the Mount of Transfiguration when Jesus' glory was revealed and Moses and Elijah appeared (Matt. 17): 'For when he received honor and glory from God the Father, and the voice was borne to him by the Majestic Glory' (2 Pet. 1 v. 17a). Peter couldn't have been any more certain for himself that he was established in the truth of God's precious and great promises. Those ancient promises from the Lord of glory he saw face-to-face. He wants you and me to have that assurance.

## The Certainty of Peter's Ear Witness

Then Peter continues his argument with the certainty of his ear witness. He not only *saw* Jesus transfigured in glory, but he *heard* the voice of God the Father from heaven. That voice testified about the truth of who Jesus was: 'This is my beloved Son, with whom I am well pleased.' Peter commented, saying, 'we ourselves [Peter, James, and John] heard this very voice borne from heaven, for we were with him on the holy mountain' (vv. 17b-18). Note well what Peter is saying. The Father's voice was as certain as the mountain up which Peter climbed and upon which Peter stood with Jesus. Peter's faith and our faith is not founded on 'cleverly devised myths' (v. 16), which are made-up stories. It's based in history, in reality, and the tangibility that Peter's feet got dirty and his muscles burned calories to get up the mountain! This is what John says in 1 John 1: 'That which was from the beginning, which we have heard, which we have seen with our eyes, which we have looked upon and have touched with our hands, concerning the word of life' (1 John 1:1).

Peter heard the God of glory whom Israel heard at Mount Sinai. He heard a distinct voice. He heard distinct words. He heard a distinct testimony about the Jesus he was following, listening to, and believing in. He wanted his hearers – us – to know this certain sound of the voice of our heavenly Father. How? Where?

## The Supra-Certainty of the Prophet's Fulfilled Witness

This leads to Peter's climax. After all Peter says so certainly because of his specific and peculiar experience as an apostle who saw and heard, there was something 'more fully confirmed' or sure (v. 19). This gives us total confidence that we've been established in the truth of God's promises: the fulfillment of the Old Testament prophets. For example, Isaiah prophesied the Messiah would be born of a virgin (Isa. 7:14). The word he used—'*alma*—was a young, unmarried woman and was the closest word Isaiah had for a 'virgin.' This is why the Septuagint (LXX) translators rendered it into Greek as *parthenos*.[4] What do we read in the Gospels? Jesus was born

---

4. For a discussion of these issues, see Gordon J. Wenham, "'BETÛLÃH 'A Girl of Marriageable Age.'" *Vetus Testamentum* 22 (1972): 326–48. See also Edward J. Young, *The Book of Isaiah: Chapters 1–18* (Grand Rapids: Eerdmans, 2000); J. Alec Motyer, *Isaiah,* Tyndale Old Testament Commentaries (Downers Grove, IL: InterVarsity Press, 1999), 378–79; John L. Mackay, *Isaiah: Volume 1, Chapters 1–39,* EP Study Commentary (Darlington: Evangelical Press, 2008), 183–85.

of Mary, a virgin (Matt. 1:23; Luke 1:27, 34). Micah prophesied the Messianic king would be born in Bethlehem (Mic. 5:2). God orchestrated history under Caesar Augustus so that Joseph and Mary moved from Nazareth in the north of Galilee to Bethlehem in Judea so that they could be taxed under Caesar's decree (Matt. 2:1, 4-6; Luke 2:1-7). David and Isaiah prophesied various aspects of the Messiah's death (Ps. 22; Isa. 52:13-53:12). The Gospels chronicle their fulfillment (cf. Matt. 26-27).

This term, 'more fully confirmed' or 'more sure,' (*bebaioteron*) is a vivid one. The NIV and NASB translate it as '*made* more sure,' but 'made' is not in the Greek text. The point Peter is making is that the Old Testament Scriptures *are* more certain and sure; they are not *made* so.[5] This word is used in several places in the New Testament. In Hebrews 6:19 it is used of a secure anchor for our souls. In 2 Corinthians 1:7 it is used of our certain hope. In Romans 4:16 it is used of the certain promise to Abraham that he was justified by faith. In Hebrews 3:6 and 3:14 it is used of our certain confidence. In Hebrews 9:17 it is used of how a last will and testament being valid ('takes effect') only upon the death of the testator. Here in 2 Peter, just before our text in 1:10, Peter uses this word not of '*making* your calling and election *sure*,' but of '*confirm*[ing] your calling and election.'[6]

Recognize what Peter is saying. The prophetic Scriptures of the Old Testament that pointed forward to Jesus Christ *are* more certain for us than the 'cleverly devised myths' (v. 16), than Peter's apostolic eyewitness, and even than the testimony of God he heard on the Mount of Transfiguration.[7] What Peter is saying is that in comparison with the prophetic word in the Old Testament as it was promised, we now have the total certainty and confidence that those prophecies have been fulfilled in the person and work of the Lord Jesus Christ.[8] All the criticisms of the Scriptures that say they

---

5.    See Simon J. Kistemaker, *Peter and Jude* (Grand Rapids: Baker, 1987), 269.

6.    'βέβαιος.' Walter Bauer, William F. Arndt, F. Wilbur Gingrich, and Frederick W. Danker, *A Greek-English Lexicon of the New Testament and Other Early Christian Literature* (Second ed., Chicago: University of Chicago Press, 1979), 138, col. 1.

7.    Alexander Nisbet, *1 & 2 Peter* (1982; repr., Edinburgh: The Banner of Truth, 1995), 239.

8.    For this last view, see D. M. Lloyd-Jones, *Expository Sermons on 2 Peter* (1983; repr., Edinburgh: The Banner of Truth, 1999), 102-03; R. C. Sproul, *1–2 Peter* (Wheaton: Crossway, 2011), 233-34. This is a nuanced difference than that of Calvin, who said the 'something more sure' was the Old Testament prophecies. *The*

are only human writings ultimately fail because of this prophetic fulfillment. The Bible is the anvil upon which the hammers of critics have and will be broken. We have something 'more fully confirmed' or *sure* (v. 19) – the prophetic word in their fulfillment and confirmation. This is why Martin Luther (1483–1546) said of this passage: 'A prophet eminently should be he who preaches Jesus Christ. Therefore, although many prophets in the Old Testament have foretold things to come, yet they came and were sent by God for this reason especially: that they should foretell of Christ.'[9]

What is said of the words of the prophets is true of all the words that God has given, as a part of the whole.[10] The Old Testament prophesied the coming of the Lord and the New Testament is the chronicle of His coming. This is why one writer said: 'The written Word, believed to be the Lord's mind, is the surest ground for faith to rest upon of any that ever has been or can be given to sinners who are subject to forgetfulness, jealousies and mistakes.'[11]

What certainty! What confidence! What assurance we have that God has spoken! God has spoken in the books of the Old and New Testaments. In saying this, Peter does not say that this certainty of God's revelation of Himself is found anywhere else. Consider this: Rome says that Peter was the first Pope. If so, why does he say the *Scriptures* are the surest foundation that we have been established

---

*Epistle of Paul the Apostle to the Hebrews and The First and Second Epistles of St Peter,* trans. William B. Johnston, eds. David W. Torrance and Thomas F. Torrance, Calvin's Commentaries, 12 vols. (Grand Rapids: Eerdmans, 1963), 12:340. Thomas Adams says this speaks of the prophets in comparison to the evangelists, as a foundation to an edifice, as Peter's Jewish audience had the Old Testament Scriptures but not the New Testament Scriptures. *A Commentary on the Second Epistle General of St. Peter,* rev. James Sherman (1839; repr., Ligonier, PA: Soli Deo Gloria, 1990), 187 col. 2-188 col. 1.

9. Martin Luther, *Commentary on Peter & Jude,* ed. John N. Lenker (1904; repr., Grand Rapids: Kregel, 1990), 247.

10. Nisbet, *1 & 2 Peter,* 238.

11. Ibid., 239.

in the truth? Why didn't he as Pope reflect back and say, 'believe me, my eyewitness to Jesus' Transfiguration is all you need? Why doesn't he say his words as Pope and the rock upon which Christ would build His Church are all that we need? Where does Peter ever appeal to himself as the final interpreter of Scripture? Peter says it is certain that *God* has spoken in Scripture, not that he as a mere man is the only interpreter of that Word. Pope Paul VI (1897–1978), though, decreed at the Second Vatican Council in 1965, that

> ...it is not from Sacred Scripture alone that the Church draws her certainty about everything which has been revealed. Therefore both sacred tradition and Sacred Scripture are to be accepted and venerated with the same sense of loyalty and reverence.[12]

Peter never said anything about his authoritative decree or the passing down of holy tradition being the foundation of faith. Instead, because of the certainty of the Word taught here, Peter tells us to 'pay attention' to these words 'as to a lamp shining in a dark place'

(v. 19). Devote yourself to the Word's light in this dark world. For how long? Until the coming of Jesus Christ when He will again shine as the light of the world on the last day: 'until the day dawns and the morning star rises in your hearts' (v. 19). Between Jesus' two comings, Peter says that this age is to be one in which you and I stick to Scripture above all! As John Calvin (1509–1564) said, 'All are immersed in darkness who do not look to the light of the Word. Therefore, unless you want to cast yourself of your own accord into a labyrinth, you must take the utmost care not to deviate even

---

12.    *Dei Verbum*, 2.9. As found at http://www.vatican.va/archive/hist_councils/ii_vatican_council/documents/vat-ii_const_19651118_dei-verbum_en.html (Accessed January 22, 2021). See also *Catechism of the Catholic Church* 82 (New York: Doubleday 1995), 31. This catechism may also be accessed at http://www.vatican.va/archive/ENG0015/_INDEX.HTM (Accessed January 25, 2021).

a hair's breadth from the direction of the Word.'[13] Outside of the Word, our faith is in a labyrinth.

## Conclusion

There's so much uncertainty and instability in our world today. There always has been. Are you confident you have a sure guide in the darkness? That guide is the living light of God Himself as He's revealed Himself in the Scriptures. He's our pillar of cloud and fire in our pilgrimage in this life. We know so because He's spoken. His Word is sure. Because He surely speaks in His Word, your faith in Him can be sure as well.

---

13.    John Calvin, *The Epistle of Paul the Apostle to the Hebrews and The First and Second Epistles of St Peter*, trans. William B. Johnston, eds. David W. Torrance and Thomas F. Torrance, Calvin's New Testament Commentaries (Grand Rapids: Wm. B. Eerdmans Publishing Company, 1963), 12:342.

# Chapter 3    REVELATION

## *He Has Spoken to Us*

'Long ago, at many times and in many ways, God spoke to our fathers by the prophets, but in these last days he has spoken to us by his Son' (Heb. 1:1-2a).

Have you ever had that experience of not seeing or knowing something, but then, as we sometimes say, 'the light turned on'? Or think of an infant. Do you know that the brain develops in such a way that when a parent plays peek-a-boo, the infant brain thinks its mom or dad really disappear? Then all of a sudden it thinks the parent reappears? Jean Piaget called this 'object permanence.'[1] When I was a young Christian, I read my Bible, including Hebrews 1:1-2, but as soon as I turned the page it was as if it was gone. Then one day 'the light turned on' for me. Why? We read, 'God spoke to our fathers,' and we say, 'Of course, they were the holy patriarchs and prophets who "saw" the Lord' (Exod. 33; Isa. 6). Then the light went on for me: 'but in these last days he has spoken *to us*.'

The fact that God has spoken means that Christianity is a revealed religion; it is a religion of revelation.[2] Revelation

---

1.    https://dictionary.apa.org/object-permanence (Accessed January 7, 2021).

2.    On revelation, see J.I. Packer, *God Has Spoken* (second revised edition, Grand Rapids: Baker Books, 1994); Peter Jensen, *The Revelation of God*, Contours of Christian Theology (Downers Grove: InterVarsity Press, 2002).

(*apokalupsis*) is a disclosure or unveiling of something previously hidden or unknown.[3] For example, in Ephesians 3:4-5 Paul speaks about 'the mystery of Christ, which was not made known to the sons of men in other generations as it has now been revealed to his holy apostles and prophets by the Spirit.' He makes three contrasts: between (1) 'the sons of men' and 'holy apostles and prophets'; (2) 'in other generations' and 'now'; and (3) 'not made known' and 'been revealed.'[4] The means 'by' which this revelation has been made known is 'the Spirit.' What is the mystery? 'This mystery is that the Gentiles are fellow heirs, members of the same body, and partakers of the promise in Christ Jesus through the gospel' (Eph. 3:6). The great overarching wonder of our revealed religion is this: humanity does not find God, but God finds us – Jew and Gentile – and speaks to us so that we become sons (and daughters) in His only begotten Son.[5]

We believe that the Scriptures are the revelation of God. He opens His mind and heart and expresses Himself to us in spoken and written words. What we learn from Hebrews 1:1-2 is that *over the ages God has revealed Himself to His people through the spoken Word and especially in the written Word.* I want to ask three questions from our text.

## Who Is the God That Speaks?

The first question I want to ask is this: *who is the God that speaks?* 'Long ago, at many times and in many ways, *God* spoke to our fathers by the prophets, but in these last days *he* has spoken to us **by** *his* **Son**.' Obviously, the apostolic writer says the speaker is *God*. The Jewish Scriptures begin by saying He's the Creator: 'in the beginning God created the heavens and the earth' (Gen. 1:1). He revealed Himself to Father Abram as 'God Almighty,' *El Shaddai* (אֵל שַׁדַּי; Gen. 17:1). He revealed Himself to Moses as 'the God of your father, the God of Abraham, the God of Isaac, and the God of Jacob' (Exod. 3:6) and as 'I AM WHO I AM' (אֶהְיֶה אֲשֶׁר אֶהְיֶה; 3:14). Over and over again to the prophets He revealed Himself as 'the LORD of Hosts' (יְהוָה צְבָאוֹת; e.g., Isa. 6:3). Yet what the inspired

---

3.   'ἀποκάλυψις.' Bauer, Arndt, Gingrich, and Danker, *Greek-English Lexicon,* 92 col. 1-2.

4.   This is the aorist passive indicative verb ἀπεκαλύφθη, from ἀποκάλυπτω. See Bauer, Arndt, Gingrich, and Danker, *Greek-English Lexicon,* 92 col. 1.

5.   *Catechism of the Catholic Church* 52, p. 24.

author highlights in Hebrews 1:1 is the fact that this God *spoke*. As with Ephesians 3 above, note well the series of comparisons and contrasts: (1) 'long ago' and 'in these last days,' (2) 'to our fathers' and 'us,') and (3) 'by the prophets' and 'by his Son.' What unites what happened then and now? *God* spoke. Whether in the past through prophets or in the last days through His Son, *God* spoke.

Has the light gone on for what this means? Our God is personal. We have a God who speaks. He speaks in words we humans can understand. How is this so? As Christians with both our Old and New Testaments opened before us ('us' being the cloud of witnesses of the historic catholic Church), we believe this personal speech is rooted in the fact that our God is tri-personal. Because God is Father, Son, and Holy Spirit, He speaks. Think of it like this: 'in the beginning' (Gen. 1:1) when 'God said...and it was so' (Gen. 1:6, 7) and when He later 'spoke *to* our fathers *by* the prophets,' this speech 'outside' of Himself in the world implies a prior 'speech' among Himself or 'inside' as Triune. To say that God speaks to us takes us back to the revealed reality that the persons of the Holy Trinity have communed with one another from all eternity and for all eternity. Jesus used the figure of speech (John 10:6) that He was a shepherd and His disciples were His sheep, that they knew His voice and He called them all by name (John 10:3-5), and that He knew them and they knew Him (John 10:14). This knowing was analogous to the Father and Son's knowing one another: 'I know my own and my own know me, *just as* (the comparative adverb, *kathōs*)[6] the Father knows me and I know the Father' (John 10:14-15a). Now He has spoken to us! This mutual 'knowing' of one another as Father and Son, Jesus described in His famous prayer to the Father as a giving to the Son a work to accomplish (John 17:4), as a sharing of eternal glory (John 17:5), a giving to Him of a people (John 17:6), and a giving to Him words to give to others (John 17:8).

Turn back to Genesis 1 to see this personalness of God in the creation story. In the six days of creation, we read ten times of God speaking, and of something coming into being (Gen. 1:3, 6, 9 [2x], 11, 14, 20 [2x], 24, 26). We call these speech acts God's *fiats*. With the creation of humanity, we read in Genesis 1:28 that God pauses and has a conversation, which Christians have traditionally made

---

6. 'καθὼς.' Bauer, Arndt, Gingrich, and Danker, *Greek-English Lexicon*, 391 col. 1-2.

sense of via the doctrine that the one God is tri-personal.[7] The very creation of man was a personal act. Then we read that after God made Adam, He revealed His will to Adam in 2:16. The important truth to take away from this is that if revelation was necessary for humanity before the fall into sin, how much more so now after the fall into sin with all its effects upon our knowledge of God?

This truth is also taught to us in Romans 1. Paul says God reveals Himself in the creation (cf. Ps. 19) and that everyone knows this. In this creation-speech, God reveals His existence and power, but not His grace. He reveals that He is the Creator but not that He is the Redeemer. This means something more is needed for the knowledge of salvation. Another *kind* of revelation is required that humans cannot acquire naturally.[8] That something else is His revealed Word of gospel, good news.

We need God to reveal Himself in a personal way so that we can know Him. This comes to us in the Scriptures. One theological forefather, Francis Turretin (1623–1687), once said this about Scripture: 'Without it the Church could not now stand. So, God indeed was not bound to the Scriptures, but he has bound us to them.'[9] This means God accommodates Himself to us as His creatures in Scripture. Like a father or mother communicates to their children first in words and then in writing, so too God first spoke to His people and then had His words

FRANCISCVS TVRRETTINVS
THEOLOGVS GENEVENSIS
*Obijt* XXVIII *Septemb. Anno* MDCLXXXVII
*Annos natus* LXIII *Mens* XI *Dies* XI .

---

7.    For example, the Belgic Confession, article 9, says in part, 'In the book of Genesis God says, "Let us make man in our image, according to our likeness." So "God created man in his own image" – indeed, "male and female he created them." "Behold, man has become like one of us." It appears from this that there is a plurality of persons within the Deity, when he says, "Let us make man in our image" – and afterwards he indicates the unity when he says, "God created." It is true that he does not say here how many persons there are – but what is somewhat obscure to us in the Old Testament is very clear in the New.'

8.    *The Catechism of the Catholic Church* 50 also says, '...there is another order of knowledge, which man cannot possibly arrive at by his own powers...' (p. 23).

9.    Francis Turretin, *Institutes of Elenctic Theology*, trans. George Musgrave Giger, ed. James T. Dennison, Jr., 3 vols. (Phillipsburg: P&R, 1992), 1:57.

passed down in writing. As John Calvin put it, like how a nurse 'lisps' to an infant, so God speaks down to our level in Scripture.[10]

## To Whom Does God Speak?

The second question I want to ask is *to whom does God speak?* 'God spoke to our *fathers*...he has spoken to *us*' (Heb 1:1, 2).

### God Spoke to Our Fathers

As we read in Hebrews 1:1, God did so 'at many times and in many ways.' He spoke in the heavens and of His power and handiwork (Ps. 19:1; cf. Rom. 1:19–20). He spoke in theophanies, that is, in revelations of Himself in the form of a human being. For example, three men visited Abraham's tent and he bowed down and said, 'O Lord, if I have found favor in your sight, do not pass by your servant' (Gen. 18:3). When we read of these men speaking, the text interestingly says, '*They* said to him' (Gen. 18:9), but also '*The* LORD said' (Gen. 18:10, 13, 14, 17) and '*I* will go down to see' (Gen. 18:21). He spoke through a voice from heaven. For example, while the liberated Israelites camped around Mount Sinai, the Lord spoke to them from it (Deut. 4:36). He spoke to Balaam through a donkey (Num. 22). He spoke through visions. For example, when the prophets like Isaiah 'saw the LORD high and lifted up,' this was in a vision (Isa. 6). He spoke through dreams. For example, in contrast to Moses whom the Lord spoke to 'face to face,' the prophets received revelation in dreams (Num. 12:6-8). He spoke through supernatural handwriting. For example, the Lord engraved the Ten Commandments with His own 'finger' (Exod. 31:18; Deut. 9:10) and when King Belshazzar praised the gods of gold, silver, bronze, iron, wood, and stone, the Lord wrote a message of doom on the wall of the palace: MENE, MENE, TEKEL, PARSIN (Dan. 5:25). He spoke through angels to deliver the message of salvation. For example, the Lord sent the angel Gabriel to proclaim the virgin birth of the Son of God to Joseph and Mary (Matt. 1:20-21; Luke 1:26-33).

### God Has Spoken to Us

He's also spoken in this era of the New Covenant. Let me state the obvious but stupendous truth: He speaks to sinners! Don't forget this: because we're sinners, our knowledge of God is not as it should be.

---

10. John Calvin, *Institutes of the Christian Religion*, trans. John Allen, 2 vols. (Philadelphia: Presbyterian Board of Christian Education, 1936), 1.13.1.

Even as believers we see only 'in a mirror dimly' (1 Cor. 13:12). Even worse is the knowledge of God we had when we were unbelievers. I'll summarize with a quote from the Canons of Dort (1618–19).[11] Consider the third and fourth head of doctrine, article 1. It first speaks of humanity's original creation in terms of mind, will, and affections: 'Man was originally created in the image of God and was furnished in his *mind with a true and salutary knowledge of his Creator and things spiritual*; in his will and heart with righteousness, and in all his emotions with purity; indeed, the whole man was holy.' In contrast, because of Adam's original sin 'he deprived himself of these outstanding gifts. Rather, in their place he brought upon himself *blindness, terrible darkness, futility, and distortion of judgment in his mind*; perversity, defiance, and hardness in his heart and will, and finally impurity in all his emotions.'

To be blind means you can't see. Most of us don't have that experience, but you've probably put on a blindfold or been in a really dark room where you could not see. The Bible says that is what it is like for us as sinners to understand God. We cannot see Him rightly. 'But God!' (Eph. 2:4). Like Jesus healed a man born blind, who responded, 'One thing I do know, that though I was blind, now I see' (John 9:25), so with us spiritually. Again, to summarize, let me cite another article from the Canons of Dort:

> ...when God carries out this good pleasure in his chosen ones, or works true conversion in them, he not only sees to it that the gospel is proclaimed to them outwardly, and *enlightens their minds* powerfully by the Holy Spirit so that they may *rightly understand and discern the things of the Spirit of God*, but, by the effective operation of the same regenerating Spirit, he also penetrates into the inmost being of man, opens the closed heart, softens the hard heart, and circumcises the heart that is uncircumcised. He infuses new qualities into the will, making the dead will alive, the evil one good, the unwilling one willing, and the stubborn one compliant; he activates and strengthens the will so that, like a good tree, it may be enabled to produce the fruits of good deeds (3/4.11).

---

11.    For an introduction and commentary on the Canons, see my *Grace Worth Fighting For: Recapturing the Vision of God's Grace in the Canons of Dort* (Lincoln, NE: Davenant Institute, 2019).

Eene vergadering van de nationale Synode te Dordrecht

What happens when you pull a blindfold off or turn on a light in a dark room? You can see. How does that happen to us spiritually? The Holy Spirit is that light. For us to understand the Word, Paul says in 1 Corinthians 2 that we need the Spirit of God to illumine our darkened understanding even as believers.

## Why Does God Speak?

Finally, let me ask a third question: *why does God speak?* When we read Hebrews 1:1-2 along with verse 14, which speaks of 'inherit[ing] salvation,' and 2:3, which speaks of our having 'such a great salvation,' it becomes clear why God 'spoke to our fathers' and why 'he has spoken to us' in words and writing: to bring us into a saving relationship with Him. Let me cite for you a wonderful quote from J. I. Packer: 'He speaks to us simply to fulfill the purpose for which we were made; that is, to bring into being a relationship in which He is a friend to us, and we to Him, He finding His joy in giving us gifts and we finding ours in giving Him thanks.'[12]

We see this expressed in the Protestant Reformation doctrinal statement, the Belgic Confession, which says of the Word God inspired through holy prophets and apostles: 'Afterwards our God – because of the special care he has for us and our salvation – commanded his servants, the prophets and apostles, to commit

---

12.    J. I. Packer, *God Has Spoken* (1965; rev. ed., London: Hodder and Stoughton, 1979), 28-50.

this revealed Word to writing' (art. 3). The Latin text says it even more strongly: 'afterwards, *in truth/in fact/certainly*[13] God from a *unique/singular*[14] care' (*vero Deus, pro singulari cura*).[15] God has come down to our level and spoken to us in our weakness in His immeasurable care and concern for us. Like Calvin said, as parents make cooing sounds and eat some baby food before giving it to their children, so God has accommodated Himself to us in language we can understand in the written Word. Calvin also said that since the revelation of God in the creation is insufficient to bring us to God, 'we need another and better assistance...the light of his word, to make himself known unto salvation, and hath honoured with this privilege those whom he intended to unite in a more close and familiar connection with himself.'[16]

To be friends, there must be communication between two people. There must be conversation. Concerning God and us, the words from Him to us are mediated through paper and ink, but one day the words will be communicated directly face to face (1 Cor. 13:12; Rev. 22:4). Let me illustrate this. When I was a kid my favorite baseball player was Reggie Jackson when he was with the Angels. I knew all about him from his baseball cards (we couldn't Google his name and read a Wikipedia article!). I had a poster of him. I listened to him being interviewed on the radio as I tuned in to games. I even remember the one year our little league was allowed to walk on the field before a game. As we walked past the dugout, there he was. I tried to yell out, 'Reggie,' but he must not have heard me. Then during the pre-game warm-ups I crowded along the outfield wall yelling out to him for an autograph, for him to toss me a ball, anything. What did I get in return? Nothing.

## Conclusion: 'I have found the Book!'

Let me conclude by saying that God has revealed Himself to us in His written Word. When we realize this, the light should go on in our minds and hearts. Think about the story of the great and

---

13.   Leo F. Stelten, *Dictionary of Ecclesiastical Latin* (1995; Peabody, MA: Hendrickson Publishers, sixth printing 2004), 284.

14.   Ibid., 248.

15.   De Nederlandse Belijdensgeschriften, ed. J.N. Bakhuizen van den Brink (Amsterdam: Uitgeverij Ton Bolland, 1976), 73. See my *With Heart and Mouth: An Exposition of the Belgic Confession* (Grandville, MI: Reformed Fellowship, 2008), 70.

16.   Calvin, *Institutes*, 1.6.1.

godly king of Judah called Josiah. In 2 Kings 22–23 we read of his reforms in the life of the people of God. Why did he repent? Why did he change the church's course of action and affection? We read in 2 Kings 22:8 that when the temple was being repaired from its ruinous state, Hilkiah the high priest found a copy of the law of Moses in the temple. His exact words were this: 'I have found the Book of the Law.'

When we realize that what we have in what we call the Word of God are the very words of God (*ipsissima verba Dei*), then everything begins to change for us. We begin to repent when we read His laws. We begin to rejoice when we read His gospel. What does this have to do with our disagreement with the Roman and Orthodox Churches? The main application is that if God truly has revealed Himself in His Word to bring sinners into covenant with Him, we don't need another authority equal to the Word, whether a Pope or a church's Tradition. When that light goes on, we can hear the living and active voice of our gracious God in the words He sent us from heaven.

# Chapter 4   INSPIRATION
## *Breathed Out by God*

'All Scripture is breathed out by God and profitable for teaching, for reproof, for correction, and for training in righteousness' (2 Tim. 3:16).

In 1957, E. J. Young, a Professor of Old Testament at Westminster Seminary in Philadelphia, wrote; 'To say that Christianity is now at cross-roads is to engage in the trite and the commonplace.'[1] If that was true then with twentieth-century theological liberalism, it's true now with so-called postmodernism's infection in the Church. It seems that every generation needs to have their own battle for the Bible against enemies outside as well as inside the Church. Those inside struggles are what we historic Protestants still have with Roman Catholics and Orthodox Christians.

---

1.    E. J. Young, *Thy Word is Truth* (1957; repr., Edinburgh: The Banner of Truth, 1997), 13. For an excellent study of an historic Lutheran view of inspiration, see Robert Preuss, *The Inspiration of Scripture: A Study of the Theology of the Seventeenth Century Lutheran Dogmaticians* (1955; Edinburgh and London: Oliver and Boyd, second edition 1957).

Yet the doctrine of the inspiration of Scripture is one of the basic truths about the Word of God that all historic Christians affirm.[2] Second Timothy 3:16 is one of the basic texts where the doctrine is found. It teaches that *we receive, believe, preach, read, and seek to live in obedience to the Word of God because it is the very words of God to us.* This builds in us confidence since the words of God inscripturated by pen and paper have a quality that no human writings, or human leaders like the Pope, or human Tradition like that in Orthodoxy, have.

## What Inspiration Is Not

Let me first explain *what inspiration is not.*

When we say the Scriptures are inspired, we are not saying that the authors were inspired to write so that they would merely move their readers' souls religiously, spiritually, or emotionally. The Scriptures *should*, but there's more to it. The inspiration of Scripture doesn't mean the same thing as when we say we felt inspired after reading a poem or hearing a moving speech. This view says the Holy Spirit only affected the writers and not their writings. Therefore, inspiration is understood to be a literary or religious 'inspiration.'

When we say the Scriptures are inspired, we're not saying that they become the Word of God as we encounter them. When we read or hear the Word, especially as it's preached, we *should* hear God's voice confronting us in law and comforting us in gospel. But that's not all. This view is the so-called neo-orthodox view of Karl Barth and his followers, the Barthians, that says in the 'crisis' of encountering the Word of God, it comes alive and affects us in a certain way. This places inspiration, again, in persons, and not in the words themselves.

Finally, when we say the Scriptures are inspired, we're not saying that Scripture contains the Word of God like corn in a husk. Some say that it is inspired in its theological and ethical teaching but that it cannot be trusted on issues like the days of creation, its history, archaeology, and chronology. For example, there is a novel view today that says we believe that Genesis 1–2 teaches that God created everything; but this is all that it says. This view says that

---

2. For Roman Catholic affirmation, see *Catechism of the Catholic Church* 105–108, pp. 36-37. For Orthodox affirmation, see Bradley Nassif and Edward Rommen, *Three Views on Eastern Orthodoxy and Evangelicalism*, eds. Stanley Gundry and James Stamoolis, Counterpoints (Grand Rapids: Zondervan, 2004), 36-37, 236-37.

the rest we should leave to science. Therefore, 'Adam' was a product of evolutionary process since we all know evolution is fact! But the Scriptures never say to us, 'Don't listen to this part'; instead, it speaks with authority in all its parts and assumes that all its parts come from God.

## What Inspiration Is

Let me now explain *what inspiration is*.

In the words of the apostle Paul, *all Scripture is breathed out by God* (2 Tim. 3:16). In context, the *Scriptures* are the writings of the human prophets to other humans using human language. Yet they've been *breathed out by God*. Paul uses a term used nowhere else in the New Testament to express this: *theopneustos*.[3] Paul is saying that the Scriptures come directly from God or 'of God,' as the King James translation puts it. These two realities don't mean the Scriptures are the Word of God and the word of man, but the Word of God *through* the word of man. Athanasius (196/198–373) described this divine inspiration through human authors as 'a common grace of the Spirit in all, and let it be found existing in each one, the same grace among all, whenever the need demands and the Spirit desires...as each unstintingly accomplishes and completes its own service.'

He went on to warn his readers not to change the words of the Psalms so that when they were sung and chanted 'just as they are spoken...the holy men who supplied these, recognizing that which is their own, to join you in your prayer, or, rather, so that even the Spirit who speaks in the saints, seeing words inspired by him in them, might render assistance to us.'[4]

As a Jewish rabbi, Paul drew his teaching in part from the Old Testament. Listen to the similar imagery from Deuteronomy 8,

3.　'θεόπνευστος.' See Bauer, Arndt, Gingrich, and Danker, *Greek-English Lexicon*, 356 col. 2.

4.　Athanasius, 'Letter to *Marcellinus* on the Interpretation of the Psalms,' 10, 31 in *Athanasius: The Life of Antony and the Letter to Marcellinus*, trans. Robert C. Gregg, The Classics of Western Spirituality (Malwah, NJ: Paulist Press, 1980), 107, 127.

where Moses said, 'The whole commandment' (i.e., Scripture) that I command you today you shall be careful to do…and you shall remember the whole way that the LORD your God has led you these forty years in the wilderness, that he might humble you, testing you to know what was in your heart, whether you would keep *his commandments* (i.e., Scripture) or not. And he humbled you and let you hunger and fed you with manna, which you did not know, nor did your fathers know, that he might make you know that man does not live by bread alone, but man lives by 'every word' (i.e., Scripture) 'that comes from the mouth of the LORD' (Deut. 8:1-3).

Similar to Paul's image of Scripture being *breathed out*, Moses says that the commandments and every word 'comes from *the mouth of the LORD.*' In other words, they are His very words. In Psalm 33:6 we sing in parallel lines that even as God spoke His Word and the heavens and earth were created, so He breathed and all the hosts of heaven were created.

This means that we believe in a *verbal* inspiration, that is, the very words themselves are given by God. God *breathed out* or spoke and His speech is accessible in human words. As Jesus said, even the 'iotas' (ESV) or 'jots' (KJV) and the 'dots' (ESV) or 'tittles' (KJV) are inspired (Matt. 5:18). He was speaking of the smallest strokes on the letters in the Hebrew alphabet to say God's Word is just that – *God's Word* – and therefore completely reliable. In Matthew 22:43-45 and in Galatians 3:16 entire arguments are based on the tense of a verb and the number of a word. This also means that we believe in a *plenary* inspiration, that is, that the entire words are the very words of God. It is not that only this part of the Scriptures is inspired whereas that other part is not. To use the aforementioned phrase from our forefathers, in Scripture we read and hear 'the very words of God' (*ipsissima verba Dei*).

Our Protestant forefathers said precisely what the holy catholic Church has always said in saying this. For example, one of the earliest Christian apologists, that is, defenders of the faith, was Justin Martyr (100–165). Justin said, '…when you hear the utterances of the prophets spoken as it were personally, you must not suppose that they are spoken by the inspired themselves, but by the Divine Word who moves them.'[5] One of the great Trinitarian theologians of the ancient Church, Gregory of Nyssa (335–395), said that 'all

---

5.  *First Apology 36 in Ante-Nicene Fathers*, ed. A. Cleveland Coxe, 10 vols. (1885; repr., Hendrickson Publishers, fourth printing 2004), 1:175 col. 1.

things the Divine Scripture says are utterances of the Holy Spirit.'[6] Finally, in his *Confessions*, Augustine wrote like he was having a dialog with God, in which God said to him, 'O humanity – of course what my scripture says is what I say!'[7] Scripture comes from God.

## Where Paul Learned It

Based on 2 Timothy 3, therefore, *we receive, believe, preach, read, and seek to live in obedience to the Word of God because it is the very words of God to us.* Let me further explain in terms of *where Paul learned* this doctrine.

First, Paul learned this from the Lord Jesus Christ. Our Lord over and over again affirms the Old Testament as the very words of God (e.g., Matt. 5:17; 26:53-56; Luke 18:3ff.; 22:37; 24:25ff.; 24:44ff.; John 5:39; 13:18; 15:25; 17:12). This is why He says in John 10:35 that the Scripture cannot be broken. This is why He says in Luke 16:17 that it is easier for heaven and earth to pass away than for a single stroke of one letter in the law to pass away. As Lord of the Church, Jesus approved the coming New Testament writings since He chose as His apostles those who knew Him during His entire ministry, those who witnessed His resurrection, and those whom He promised to send His Spirit upon to lead into all truth (John 14:26; 16:12-14).

Second, Paul 'learned' this from his fellow apostles. For example, Paul calls the Gospel of Luke 'Scripture' (1 Tim. 6:18). Peter puts Paul's writings on the same level as the Old Testament in 2 Peter 3:15-16. Luke, in the Book of Acts, says the apostles spoke in the Spirit (Acts 2:4; 4:8; 6:10). The Book of Hebrews speaks of the Old Testament as the words of the Spirit (Heb. 3:7) and then

---

6.   *Against Eunomius* 7:1 in *Nicene and Post-Nicene Fathers: Second Series,* ed. Philip Schaff and Henry Wace, 14 vols. (1893; repr., Hendrickson Publishers, fourth printing 2004), 5:192, col. 2.

7.   Augustine, *Confessions* 13.29.44 in *Confessions: Books 9–13,* trans. Carolyn J.–B. Hammond, Loeb Classical Library (Cambridge, MA: Harvard University Press, 2016), 413.

tells us we need to pay attention to what we have heard from Christ, the apostles, and in his letter (Heb. 2:1-4).

Third, Paul learned this from his fellow countrymen, as a trained rabbi. This is why both Romans 3:2 and Acts 7:38 describes the Jews as keepers of the 'oracles of God.' When we read the New Testament, we come to see how seriously and meticulously the leadership of Israel was with regard to the Word of God. In the midst of a rebuke of the Jewish leadership in Jerusalem, Jesus praised them, 'You search the Scriptures because you think that in them you have eternal life' (John 5:39a).

Fourth, Paul learned this from the Old Testament itself. The prophets' own witness is key here. They were conscious of bringing the word of the Lord: 'Thus says the LORD' is used hundreds of times (e.g., Jer. 36:27).

## Conclusion: So What?

Let me conclude by asking so what? Why does this matter? In other words, what happens when we lose this doctrine of inspiration? In his book *God Has Spoken*, J. I. Packer offered five reasons why this is important in terms of what we lose if we reject the Bible's own doctrine of inspiration.[8]

First, preaching is undermined. If Scripture is not breathed out as 2 Timothy 3 says, then preachers become something other than proclaimers and heralds of the words of God. Preachers become entertainers, stand-up comics, or therapists.

Second, teaching is undermined. If Scripture is not breathed out as we have seen it from 2 Timothy 3, then what are we to teach? In the end, we will ask Pilate's sad question, 'What is truth?' Then we will end up defining truth for ourselves in merely relativistic terms like our culture: 'This morning I'm going to speak *my* truth.'

Third, faith is weakened. If Scripture is not breathed out as we have seen, then there is nothing sure to cling to by faith in the struggles and temptations of life. Where do we go for strength in storms? God? How do you know you can go to Him? How do you know where to find Him?

Fourth, Bible reading is discouraged. If Scripture is not breathed out as we have seen it, then why read it? It's no different than *Aesop's*

---

8. Packer, *God Has Spoken*, 28-30.

*Fables*, Greek and Roman mythology, John Donne's (1572–1631) poetry, or Langston Hughes' (1902–1967) poetry.

Fifth, Christ is hidden from view. If Scripture is not breathed out as above, then Jesus is not 'publicly portrayed as crucified' before His people (Gal. 3:1); He is not the sum and substance of the various genres and books of the Bible; and He becomes a merely mortal example to follow.

While we agree with Rome and Orthodoxy that the Old and New Testaments are inspired by God, yet Rome and Orthodoxy insist on unwritten traditions as equally authoritative. J. C. Ryle (1816–1900) once asked the simple question we are asking, 'Is the Bible the Word of God?' He then said, 'Let us regard all who would damage the authority of the Bible, or impugn its credit, as spiritual robbers.' Why? 'We are traveling through a wilderness: they rob us of our only **guide**. We are voyaging over a stormy sea: they rob us of our only **compass**. We are toiling over a weary road: they pluck our **staff** out of our hands.' Of these robbers, he concluded:

> And what do these spiritual robbers give us in place of the Bible? What do they offer as a safer guide and better provision for our souls? Nothing! Absolutely nothing! Big swelling words! Empty promises of new light! High sounding jargon; but nothing substantial and real! They would willingly take from us the bread of life, and they do not give us in its place so much as a stone. Let us turn a deaf ear to them. Let us firmly grasp and prize the Bible more and more, the more it is assaulted.[9] God has spoken—'breathed out' his words *(theopneustos)*—through prophets and apostles. Hear him. Believe him. Serve him by speaking his words to all you know.

9. J. C. Ryle, *Bible Inspiration: Its Reality and Nature* (London: William Hunt and Company, 1877), 70, 71.

# Chapter 5 AUTHORITY
## *Let Them Hear Them*

The poor man died and was carried by the angels to Abraham's side. The rich man also died and was buried, and in Hades, being in torment, he lifted up his eyes and saw Abraham far off and Lazarus at his side. And he called out, 'Father Abraham, have mercy on me, and send Lazarus to dip the end of his finger in water and cool my tongue, for I am in anguish in this flame.' But Abraham said, 'Child, remember that you in your lifetime received your good things, and Lazarus in like manner bad things; but now he is comforted here, and you are in anguish. And besides all this, between us and you a great chasm has been fixed, in order that those who would pass from here to you may not be able, and none may cross from there to us.' And he said, 'Then I beg you, father, to send him to my father's house – for I have five brothers – so that he may warn them, lest they also come into this place of torment.' But Abraham said, 'They have Moses and the Prophets; let them hear them.' And he said, 'No, father Abraham, but if someone goes to them from the dead, they will repent.' He said to him, 'If they do not hear Moses and the Prophets, neither will they be convinced if someone should rise from the dead' (Luke 16:22-31).

Jesus' illustration recorded in Luke 16 of the rich man and Lazarus in the afterlife brings home the powerful point that the Word of God is authoritative.[1] The rich man in anguish in Hades pleads with Father Abraham to send Lazarus from his comforting side back to his five brothers in this life to warn them of what awaits them in the life to come. Abraham's response to the rich man is that his brothers already *have Moses and the Prophets*, meaning, the Old Testament Scriptures. Because of this he says, *let them hear them* (Luke 16:29). The rich man insisted, though: *if someone goes to them from the dead, they will repent* (Luke 16:30). Abraham reasserted the truth: *If they do not hear Moses and the Prophets, neither will they be convinced if someone should rise from the dead* (Luke 16:31).

What's the point of this illustration? Consistent with the Old Testament prophets, Jesus points His people to the enduring authority of the Word of the living God. Moses proclaimed to Israel that in the days to come in the Promised Land, they would have disputes and legal cases among themselves. When this happened, they were to go to Jerusalem ('the place that the LORD your God will choose,' Deut. 17:8, 10), present their case to the priests and judge, and wait for their verdict. Then what? The Lord would reveal His will to them and 'you shall do all according to what they declare to you...you shall be careful to do according to all that they direct you' (Deut. 17:10). Even as God revealed Himself to Moses (Exod. 18), He would do the same through the priests and judges in days to come. Generations later, as the Word of the Lord was being codified into the canon, Isaiah called the people of God back to the Law of God. Instead of seeking out mediums and necromancers, Isaiah said, 'To the teaching and to the testimony!' (Isa. 8:20). The 'teaching' or *torah* (הְרות) was 'the revelation of God expressing His will for man's obedience' and the 'testimony' (הְדועָת) was 'His revelation expressing His will as a system to be believed.'[2] The mediums and necromancers that 'will not speak according to this word...have no dawn...will pass through the land, greatly distressed and hungry... will look to the earth, but behold, distress and darkness.... And...will be thrust into thick darkness' (Isa. 8:20,

1. For an introduction to biblical authority, see J.I. Packer, *'Fundamentalism' and the Word of God: Some Evangelical Principles* (1958; repr., Grand Rapids: Wm. B. Eerdmans Publishing Co., 1992).

2. Edward J. Young, *The Book of Isaiah: Chapters 1–18*, 3 vols. (1965; repr., Grand Rapids: William B. Eerdmans Publishing Company, 1996), 1:319.

21, 22). In other words, 'there is no hope outside of what the Lord has spoken; every utterance, however spirit-authorized, which fails to accord with his word is darkness without light.'[3]

Jesus constantly called His disciples and opponents back to the Scriptures as well: His disciples before (Luke 9:22; 18:31) and after His death and resurrection (Luke 24:25-27, 32, 44-47), the devil (Matt. 4:1-11), the Sadducees (Matt. 22:29), and the Pharisees (Matt. 22:34-40). The apostles' practice of appealing to the authority of Scripture is what Acts and the epistles are all about! As we saw in 2 Peter 1:19, Peter pointed us to the Word not to the Papacy or Tradition in himself. Paul even described the Bereans as noble because they searched the Scriptures to determine if his words to them were true (Acts 17:11).

The Scriptures therefore are authoritative. This authority is the inherent right they possess making them necessary for us to believe all that they say and to obey all that they command.[4] Remember the phrase from the Heidelberg Catechism that I cited above: 'true faith' includes 'a sure knowledge by which I hold as true all that God has revealed to us in his Word' (Q&A 21). This authority of Scripture is why the Westminster Confession says, 'it ought to be believed, and obeyed…and therefore it is to be received, because it is the Word of God' (1.4).[5]

The question I want to explore with you is *how* do we know the Scriptures are authoritative? The old debate between the Roman Catholics and Reformed catholics was and continues to be this: do we come to this persuasion *primarily* through the Church's testimony or through the testimony of the Scriptures themselves? Therefore, *secondarily* this confidence comes by means of the Church.

---

3.   J. Alec Motyer, *Isaiah: An Introduction and Commentary*, Tyndale Old Testament Commentaries (Downers Grove: Inter-Varsity Press, 1999), 86-87. 'Those who pretended to speak the word of the Lord from sources others than this have not even a glimmer of light about them' (Allan Harman, Isaiah: *A Covenant to be kept for the sake of the Church*, Focus on the Bible [2005; repr., Ross-Shire, Scotland: Christian Focus, 2011], 107. See also John L. Mackay, *Isaiah: Volume 1*, EP Study Commentary (2008; repr., Welwyn Garden City, UK: EP Books, 2018), 218.

4.   Francis Turretin defined it as, 'The right and dignity of the sacred books, on account of which they are most worthy of faith with regard to those things which they propose to be believed and of our obedience in those things they command us to omit or to do' (*Institutes*, 1:62).

5.   *Reformed Confessions: Volume 4*, 235.

## The Spirit's Witness

The Word of God clearly evidences and testifies of its own authority. This is primary according to the Scriptures themselves. The *way* the Scriptures impress this upon our heads and hearts is the Holy Spirit's witness or testimony. In the next section below we will come back to the witness of the Word itself. It is important to recognize that the Holy Spirit who inspired the Scriptures is 'behind' the Word as the cause of their authority. The Church's witness is important, too, as we will see, but it is only the means by which the Word is proclaimed so that the Spirit can do His work. He has an internal witness to us as well as an external witness in the Word itself (primary) as well as through the Church (secondary).

In Romans 8 we read of the Holy Spirit's internal testimony to our believing hearts that we are children of God. There Paul says our identity and existence is that we are not 'in the flesh' (ruled by our sinful desires) but 'in the Spirit if [*since*] in fact the Spirit of God dwells in you' (Rom. 8:9). This is why 'we are debtors' not to live according to our sinful desires (the flesh) but to live according to the Spirit's desires for us (Rom. 8:12). All who live in this way, what Paul calls being 'led by the Spirit of God,' are in fact 'sons of God' (Rom. 8:14). Paul says 'sons' because inheritance customs and laws at that time generally passed down through firstborn sons and other sons. His point is that *all* believers, whether male or female, are sons who receive an inheritance (see verse 17). As sons, we 'did not receive the spirit of slavery' but 'the Spirit of adoption as sons, by whom we cry, "Abba! Father!"' (Rom. 8:15). This Spirit, in fact, 'bears witness with our spirit that we are children of God, and if children, then heirs – heirs of God and fellow heirs with Christ' (Rom. 8:16-17). Note a twofold internal witness in verse 16: it is the Spirit who bears witness *to* us and He does so '*with* our spirit.' In the same way that the Spirit testifies that we belong with Christ to God the Father as sons, so He testifies that the words our Father has breathed out to us in Scripture are His authoritative words to us, His children. In fact, Jesus calls His words 'spirit and life' (John 6:63).

What is this inner witness of the Spirit to our spirits and with our spirits? Is it the same thing that Mormon missionaries tell you to ask God for when you read their holy texts? They speak of a 'burning in the bosom'; is this the same thing?[6] Not even close. This internal testimony of the Holy Spirit 'does not consist of ecstasy or enthusiasm. It is a certain light that is sprinkling our mind in such a way that the mind is affected softly by it, while showing the reasons implanted in the Word itself, criteria that were previously hidden.'[7] To use the language of the Westminster Confession, 'our full persuasion and assurance of the infallible truth and divine authority thereof, is from the inward work of the Holy Spirit bearing witness *by* and *with* the Word in our hearts' (I.5; emphasis added).[8]

## The Word's Own Witness

Even as the Spirit bears witness to our spirits and with our spirits, so similarly He bears witness to His Word and with His Word. Better, with His Word through His Word. This is why we say that the Word testifies of its own trustworthiness in and of itself (*autopistos*).[9] This means that the authority of Scripture is derived from its origin and source, which is God Himself. Let me illustrate by asking you to think about a diamond. Its refraction of light, its glowing brilliance in the sun, and its ability to cut glass all testify that it is a diamond. It has this ability to testify of itself.[10] As the Belgic Confession says, 'we believe without a doubt all things contained in [the canonical books]…because they prove themselves to be from God. *For even the blind themselves are able to see that the things predicted in them do happen*' (art. 5).

In what ways do the Scriptures testify of their own authority, that they are from God? The Westminster Confession is helpful

---

6. For an explanation of this from a Mormon perspective, see 'Your Bosom Shall Burn within You.' Found at https://www.churchofjesuschrist.org/manual/doctrine-and-covenants-student-manual/section-9-your-bosom-shall-burn-within-you?lang=eng (Accessed January 20, 2021) and Rachel Nielsen, 'What If I Don't Feel a Burning in the Bosom?' Found at https://www.churchofjesuschrist.org/study/new-era/2014/06/what-if-i-dont-feel-a-burning-in-the-bosom?lang=eng (Accessed January 20, 2021).

7. Johannes Maccovius, *Scholastic Discourse: Johannes Maccovius (1588–1644) on Theological and Philosophical Distinctions and Rules* (Apeldoorn, The Netherlands: Instituut voor Reformatieonderzoek, 2009), 59.

8. *Reformed Confessions: Volume 4*, 235.

9. 'autopistos (αὐτόπιστος).' Muller, *Dictionary of Latin and Greek Theological Terms*, 49.

10. 'Like a precious jewel proved itself by its effects' (Maccovius, *Scholastic Discourse*, 61).

in listing 'the many...incomparable excellencies,' but it explicitly mentions six 'arguments whereby it doth abundantly evidence itself to be the Word of God':

1. the heavenliness of the matter;
2. the efficacy of the doctrine;
3. the majesty of the style;
4. the consent of all the parts;
5. the scope of the whole (which is, to give all glory to God);
6. the full discovery it makes of the only way of man's salvation (I.5 cf. Westminster Larger Catechism, Q&A 4).[11]

First, *the heavenliness of the matter.* In the Scriptures we are not dealing with myths, with old wives' tales, or with morals to make us better people, but with a message from heaven to earth. In the Scriptures we read God's own address to us – His 'living and active' Word (Heb. 4:12). This heavenly message is that the Triune God made the world, sent the Son to redeem it, and gives His Holy Spirit as a guarantee of final consummation.

Second, *the efficacy of the doctrine.* This means that what the Word teaches actually has an effect upon our minds and hearts. The Word of God is not merely a book; it is speech – God's speech! When we listen to Him by reading the Bible, we learn what He says about sin and come to know why things are the way they are in our world today. When we learn what He says about Jesus Christ, we put our living trust in Him, not as an idea but as a Person. When we hear His laws, the Spirit causes us to seek to obey them because it is obedience to Him.

Third, *the majesty of the style.* The God who is 'robed in majesty' (Ps. 93:1) speaks in the Word. This doesn't mean that it is so incomprehensible that it has to be from another world, but that there is something elevated in the poetry and prose that evidence its divinity. This means that there is something about the doctrines as well. Human reason could not produce the Trinity, Incarnation, satisfaction, resurrection, and fulfillment of prophecy. This must be a book from another source and not from man.

Fourth, *the consent of all the parts.* The God who made the form of this world and filled it in six days to reflect His beauty and creativity also evidences Himself in the harmony of the Word He has spoken.

---

11. *Reformed Confessions: Volume 4,* 235, 300.

There is harmony in the one Bible between its two testaments. What illustrates this is that from Old to New Testament is a time span of 1,000–2,000 years. Over this period dozens of authors wrote as they were 'carried along by the Holy Spirit' (2 Pet. 1:21). Moses wrote in Hebrew, Daniel partly in Aramaic, and John in Greek. They wrote from different continents, what we call Africa, Asia, and Europe. All their words are harmonious, from prophecies to their fulfillment.

Fifth, *the scope of the whole (which is, to give all glory to God)*. God did not reveal His Word so that we would have a self-help book as a means to our own desired ends of health and wealth. The Bible is a book about God. This is why medieval Christians described the task of theology, saying, 'Theology is taught by God, teaches [about] God, and leads to God.'[12]

Sixth, *the full discovery it makes of the only way of man's salvation.* Since God has spoken and that speech is found in Scripture, it means that it is God's message of salvation to the world. No other ideology, philosophy, or theology in any holy or non-holy book offers the remedy for humanity's sin like the Bible:

- Buddhism says eliminating desire through meditation, religious practice, and/or asceticism leads to becoming eternally unconscious in nirvana.
- Confucianism says social conformity and virtuous living give you a sense of heaven on earth.
- Hinduism says salvation is the result of eliminating evil in your life, both in this life and in all the lives you will live (reincarnation), until you are pure enough to merge with Brahma, the great force.
- Islam means *submission* to the will of *Allah*. This submission is expressed in continual practice of the 'five pillars' of fasting, pilgrimage to Mecca, giving alms, prayer five times a day, and making the confession, 'There is no God but God (*Allah*) and Muhammad is the Prophet of God.' The result of performing these is paradise if *Allah* wills it for you.
- Judaism (modern) says that *Adonai* chose Israel and to be a part of it is salvation (whether in an afterlife or just this life).

---

12. *Theologia a Deo docetur, Deum docet, et ad Deum ducit.* A medieval summary of St. Thomas Aquinas, *Summa Theologica*, trans. Fathers of the English Dominican Province, 5 vols. (1911; repr., New York, NY: Christian Classics, 1981), 1.1.7.

- Shintoism says Japan fell from the heavens, the Emperor is a god, and the people are children of the gods. Japan was the center of the world (the World War II red sun with rays shining out) and its supremacy would be heaven on earth.
- Sikhism says repeating God's name and loving humanity brings you salvation.
- Taoism says heaven on earth comes through achieving balance/harmony between yin and yang.
- Zoroastrianism (an ancient religion that is still faintly existent) says salvation is the result of your struggle against evil and victory over it.

All of these have an idea of salvation, whether it's a better life now or in the afterlife. Note that in all of them 'salvation' is the result of human works. The revealed religion of the Old and New Testaments is that *God* **saves** *sinners*.

## The Church's Witness

*The authority of the Word of God is demonstrated primarily by God Himself and His Word and secondarily by the Church.* Let me come to *the Church's witness.* Turretin spoke clearly of the Church being a servant of the Word. He said, 'For the Bible with its own marks is the argument on account of which I believe.' That's our second point above. Then he said, 'The Holy Spirit is the efficient cause [the power] and principle from which I am induced to believe.' That's our first point above. Finally, he said, 'But the Church is the instrument and means through which I believe.' He summed this up like this:

> ...why...do I believe the Bible to be divine, I will answer that I do so on account of the Scripture itself which by its marks proves itself to be such. If it is asked whence or from what I believe, I will answer from the Holy Spirit who produces that belief in me. Finally, if I am asked by what means or instrument I believe it, I will answer through the Church which God uses in delivering the Scripture to me.[13]

The Holy Spirit is the one who convinces us of the authority of the Word through the Word. As a secondary means, the Church and other external witnesses help us to see this as well. But it has to

---

13.  Turretin, *Institutes*, 1:87.

be in this order: Spirit and Word and then Church.[14] This is why Ephesians 2:20 is so key to us. What we learn there is that the Church is built upon the Scriptures and it gets any authority it has from the Scriptures. The Scriptures did not come to be because of the Church. The Westminster Confession said it like this:

> We may be moved and induced by the testimony of the *church* to an high and reverent esteem of the Holy Scripture. And the heavenliness of the matter, the efficacy of the doctrine, the majesty of the style, the consent of all the parts, the scope of the whole (which is, to give all glory to God), the full discovery it makes of the only way of man's salvation, the many other incomparable excellencies, and the entire perfection thereof, are arguments whereby it doth abundantly *evidence itself* to be the Word of God: yet notwithstanding, our full persuasion and assurance of the infallible truth and divine authority thereof, is from the inward work of the *Holy Spirit* bearing witness by and with the Word in our hearts (WCF 1.5).[15]

One objection that both Roman Catholics and Orthodox Christians make to our understanding of scriptural authority is that the Church existed before Scripture; therefore, the Church and its tradition either grants to Scripture its authority or Scripture is added to the existing tradition that led the first-century Church. First, we don't discount the testimony of the Church in relation to the authority of Scripture. When the Belgic Confession says that 'we believe without a doubt all things contained in [the canonical books],' the first thing it goes on to say in terms of proof is 'not so much because the church receives and approves them as such' (art. 5). In other words, the Church's testimony matters; it's just third in line behind the witness of the Spirit and the witness of the Word itself. Yet Rome typically fires back that St. Augustine wrote that he was led by the Church to believe: 'But should you meet with a person not yet believing the gospel, how would you reply to him were he to say, "I do not believe?" For my part, I should not believe the gospel except as moved by the

---

14. Turretin even went so far as to say that the Church was an introductory and ministerial means of belief (*Institutes*, 1:87-88).

15. *Reformed Confessions: Volume 4*, 235.

authority of the Catholic Church.'[16] John Jewel (1522–71), English Bishop of Salisbury, commented:

These few poor words have been tossed…and wrung, and pressed to the uttermost, to yield out that was never in them. For hereby ye would fain prove that the authority of the Church…your church of Rome, and none other, is above the authority of God's Word; that is to say, that the creature is above the Creator that made heaven and earth.[17]

In speaking of the Church's authority, Augustine spoke of the Church's ministerial authority, meaning it has authority as a servant, as a means of bringing the gospel as found in Scripture. In other words, Augustine was saying that without the outward ministry of the Church, he would not have understood the gospel. The medieval theologian, Gregory of Rimini (d. 1358), illustrated Augustine's meaning as being the same as if 'in Christ's own day, a believer had said, "I would not believe the gospel were it not that the miracles of Christ move me to do so." In these sorts of statements one can indeed discern a certain stimulus to believe the gospel, but not some sort of first principle that would give grounds for believing in the gospel.'[18]

---

16. Non crederem evangelio, nisi me ecclesiae catholicae auctoritas commoveret. Augustine, Against the Epistle of Manichaeus Called 'Fundamental' 5:6 in Nicene and Post-Nicene-Fathers: First Series, trans. Richard Stothert, ed. Philip Schaff, 14 vols. (1887; repr., Peabody, MA: Hendrickson Publishers, fourth printing 2004), 4:131 col. 1. On this passage in Augustine, see Calvin, Institutes, 1.7.3; Vermigli, Early Writings, 182; Jon Balserak, "The Genevan Churches and the Western Church," in *A Companion to the Reformation in Geneva* (Leiden: Brill, 2021), 153–59.

17. John Jewel, (), 864. See Oberman, *Forerunners*, 56–57.

18. Cited in Marijn de Kroon, *We Believe in God and in Christ. Not in the Church: The Influence of Wessel Gansfort on Martin Bucer*, trans. Maria Sherwood Smith, Princeton Theological Seminary Studies in Reformed Theology and History (2004; first English edition, Louisville: Westminster John Knox Press, 2009), 10.

## Conclusion: One Main Application versus Rome

Let me conclude this chapter with one application versus Rome's understanding of this issue. What all this means is that the Church discerns the Word of God and distinguishes it from other false books, but the Church does not make these books the Word of God.[19]

Rome bases its whole claim upon a circular argument: why do we believe the Bible is divine? Because the Church says so. Why do we believe what the Church says? Because the Bible says it is authoritative. How do we know that this teaching of the Word is true? Because the Church says so. The circle never ends. This is why John Calvin once wrote, 'Against opposing arguments they will set up this brazen wall – who are you to question the interpretation of the Church?'[20] The Scriptures, therefore, are our highest and supreme judge in all doctrinal controversies. At the great Council of Nicea (325), Emperor Constantine (272–337) didn't appeal

to the Great Tradition, but to the Word to resolve the Church's doctrinal strife over the Son's relationship to the Father:

> For the gospels, the apostolical writing, and the oracles of the ancient prophets, clearly teach us what we ought to believe concerning the divine nature. Let, then, all contentious disputation be discarded; and let us seek in the divinely-inspired word the solution to the questions at issue.[21]

While the Church will always have error until Christ comes again (1 Cor. 11:19), we ultimately listen to God speaking in the Scriptures more than we listen to Popes, theologians and ourselves.

---

19.   Turretin, *Institutes*, 1:92

20.   John Calvin, 'Acts of the Council of Trent with the Antidote,' *Selected Works of John Calvin*, trans. Henry Beveridge, ed. Jules Bonnet, 7 vols. (Grand Rapids: Baker Books, 1983), 3:69.

21.   Theodoret, *The Ecclesiastical History*, trans. Blomfield Jackson in *Nicene and Post-Nicene Fathers: Second Series*, ed. Philip Schaff and Henry Wace, 14 vols. (1892; repr., Peabody, MA: Hendrickson Publishers, fourth printing 2004), 3:44.

As Jesus said, not even a person coming back to life after having been in heaven is needed to bring people to faith in Him. They – we – already have Moses and the Prophets and now the New Testament: let them and us hear them (Luke 16:29). In other words, you should have more confidence that God is speaking to you when you read and hear Scripture than if someone rose from the dead to tell you a message from the afterlife.

# Chapter 6   CANONICITY

## *The Law, the Prophets, and the Psalms*

And beginning with Moses and all the Prophets, he interpreted to them in all the Scriptures the things concerning himself (Luke 24:27).

Then he said to them, 'These are my words that I spoke to you while I was still with you, that everything written about me in the Law of Moses and the Prophets and the Psalms must be fulfilled.' Then he opened their minds to understand the Scriptures (Luke 24:44-45).

Walk into your local Barnes & Noble and ask an associate, 'Where can I find the section with the sacred scriptures?' What do you think would happen? They might look at you funny, but then would take you to a section with shelves of books. There you will find the *Tanach* of Judaism – the Law, the Prophets, and the Writings of the Old Testament; the *Qur'an* of Islam, and maybe even the *Hadith* for Sunni Muslims; the *Bhagavad Gita*, the *Upanishads*, and the *Vedas* of Hinduism; the *Tao-te-ching* of Taoism; *The Analects* of Confucianism; and then the Bible. There will be Roman Catholic and Eastern Orthodox versions with the so-called Apocrypha as well as Protestant versions with only the Old and New Testaments. How would you know which of all these books is the Word of God?

I have already alluded to the canon of Scripture multiple times, but let's deal with it in terms of Rome and Orthodoxy here.[1] Why is this so important? The Roman Catholic Church's Council of Trent decreed on April 8, 1546, that what are known as the apocryphal books – Esdras, Tobit, Wisdom, Ecclesiasticus, Baruch, and 1–2 Maccabees – are canonical. They went on to declare that those who do not receive the Old Testament, the New Testament, *and* the apocryphal books in the Vulgate translation of the Bible, *and* Rome's many traditions, are *anathema* – condemned.[2] Orthodoxy has never made such a decree but receives the Apocrypha all the same. The canon is important because it involves a debate between us and Rome; but it is also important in our multi-cultural world to know where we can find the very voice of God.

In the famous post-resurrection story of Luke 24, Jesus preaches to His disciples. Notice the source of His preaching: the Law, the Prophets, and the Psalms. This is the ancient Jewish distinction of the three parts of the Old Testament: *torah*, the law, *nevi'im*, the prophets, and *ketuvim*, the writings. From these three parts of the Old Testament, Jesus proclaimed His death and resurrection. There's something else too: Jesus equates the law, the prophets, and the writings with 'the Scriptures' (vv. 27, 45). In a word, the books within these divisions were canonical.

Our word *canon* comes from the ancient Greek word *kanon*, which was used for a geographic limit.[3] We might use an image of a boundary line. When opposition arose in the ancient Church regarding which books were the Word of God, the Church adapted this word to describe which books were within the canon. Thus, an ancient document known as the *Synopsis Scripturae Sacrae*,

---

1.  On the canon of the Old Testament, see William Henry Green, *General Introduction to the Old Testament: The Canon* (New York: Charles Scribner's Sons, 1899). On the canon of the New Testament, see F.F. Bruce, *The Canon of Scripture* (Downer's Grove: InterVarsity Press, 1998) and Bruce M. Metzger, *The Canon of the New Testament: Its Origin, Development, and Significance* (Oxford: Clarendon Press, 1987). For an overall discussion, see Herman Ridderbos, *Redemptive History and the New Testament Scriptures*, trans. H. De Jongste, rev. Richard B. Gaffin, Jr. (1963; second revised edition, Phillipsburg, NJ: Presbyterian and Reformed Publishing Company, 1988).

2.  *Canons and Decrees of the Council of Trent: Original Text with English Translation*, trans. H.J. Schroeder (1941; fourth printing, London: B. Herder Book Co., 1960), 17-18.

3.  'κανών.' Bauer, Arndt, Gingrich, and Danker, *Greek-English Lexicon*, 403 col. 1.

the synopsis or summary of sacred Scripture, said: 'All of our Christian Scriptures are inspired by God, and these books are not indefinite but set apart and designated as canonical.'[4] We also use the word *canon* in another sense. As William Whitaker (1548–1595) said, 'The books of scripture are called *canonical*, because they contain the standard and rule of our faith and morals.'[5] Think of a nation's laws. They exist to be the standard of what is right and wrong in a society. In the same way, the Word functions in the Church as the standard of truth and error.

So how do you and I know *which books belong in the Bible?* In particular, are the apocryphal books of the Roman Church and Orthodoxy canonical? What we learn from the Word of God is that *the canon of Scripture is closed to the apocryphal books of the Roman and Orthodox Churches.* I will give three reasons why the apocryphal books are not canonical. The first two are applications of Jesus' words in Luke 24, while the last is more theological and historical in nature.

## Jesus and the Jews Did Not Recognize Them

The first reason why we don't accept the apocryphal books is that *Jesus and the Jews did not recognize them.* We see Jesus in Luke 24 following the Jewish distinction of books within the Old Testament. What this means, then, is that He didn't consider any other books to be canonical. Against our Roman Catholic and Orthodox friends all we need to do is point them to this text and tell them that we are following Jesus.

Jesus, as a Jew, was following the tradition of the Jews. For example, the Jewish-born Roman historian, Josephus (37–100), in his book, *Against Apion*, said the same thing:

---

4. As found at www.bible-researcher.com/sss.html. (01/09/2022)

5. William Whitaker, *A Disputation on Holy Scripture,* trans. William Fitzgerald (1849; repr., Orlando: Soli Deo Gloria Publications, 2005), 27.

For we have not an innumerable multitude of books among us, disagreeing from and contradicting one another, [as the Greeks have,] but only twenty-two books, which contain the records of all the past times; which are justly believed to be divine...for during so many ages as have already passed, no one has been so bold as either to add any thing to them, to take any thing from them, or to make any change in them; but it is become natural to all Jews immediately, and from their very birth, to esteem these books to contain Divine doctrines, and to persist in them, and, if occasion be willingly to die for them (1.8).

'But Josephus mentions 22 books and not the 39 you have in your Protestant Bible.' The reason is that while we count 'the Law' the same (Genesis, Exodus, Leviticus, Numbers, Deuteronomy), at the time of Josephus the rest of the Old Testament was ordered differently: 'the Prophets' (Joshua, Judges [with Ruth], Samuel, Kings, Isaiah, Jeremiah [with Lamentations], Ezekiel, 'the Twelve' [Hosea–Malachi]), and 'the writings' (Psalms, Job, Proverbs, Song of Songs, Ecclesiastes, Esther, Daniel, Ezra-Nehemiah, Chronicles). The point is that the ancient canon is the same as ours. Thus, the Jews were esteemed in their treasuring and passing down the Old Testament. The Lord 'entrusted [them] with the oracles of God' (Rom. 3:2). Men such as St. Chrysostom said this meant that 'they had the law placed in their hands because God considered them so deserving that He entrusted to them the oracles that were brought down from heaven.'[6]

Another New Testament passage that speaks of the canonical limit of the Old Testament is Matthew 23:34-36 and its parallel in Luke 11:49-51. Here Jesus spoke words of woe upon the Pharisees because He would send them prophets and apostles, but they would kill, crucify, flog, and persecute. Because of this, 'on you may come all the righteous blood shed on earth, *from the blood of righteous Abel to the blood of Zechariah the son of Barachiah, whom you murdered between the sanctuary and the altar*' (Matt. 23:35 cf. Luke 11:51; emphasis mine). Like with Luke 24, the importance of this saying of Jesus is based on the order of the books within the Hebrew Bible. Abel's death is mentioned at the beginning of the first book, in Genesis 4; Zechariah's death is mentioned in

---

6.    St. John Chrysostom, *Homilies on Romans: Volume 1*, trans. Panayiotis Papageorgiou (Brookline, MA: Holy Cross Orthodox Press, 2013), 103-04.

2 Chronicles 24:20-22, which is the last book of the Hebrew Bible. Jesus mentions the first martyr and the last martyr of the prophets in the ordering of the Hebrew Bible.

But why didn't the Jews receive any other books into the Old Testament than those we have in our Bibles? They gave three reasons. The first was that the apocryphal books were not written in Hebrew, the language of the Jews. The apocryphal books, instead, were written in Greek, which testified to their being foreign books much later than the period of the prophets. The second reason was that all the apocryphal books came after the writing of the prophet Malachi in the fourth century B.C. Malachi's prophecy ends with the expectation of Elijah's return to herald the coming of the Lord Himself. A third reason was that the style and matter of the apocryphal books testify of their human origin and not their divine origin. Let me give you a brief list of the errors and absurdities contained in the apocrypha.[7]

- The book of *Judith* calls Nebuchadnezzar king of Nineveh, although Scripture and history call him the king of Babylon.
- The book of *Wisdom* attributes the Olympics to the days of Solomon (who reigned 970–930 B.C.), although they did not exist until the days of the Greek Empire.
- In the book, *Bel and the Dragon*, Daniel proves to the king that his god is really no god at all, only a fierce dragon. He proves this by showing that the king's god does not eat the daily food offerings laid before his idol statue, but a dragon does, by laying out indigestible cake, which kills the dragon. As a result, Daniel is thrown into the lions' den.
- In the book of *Tobit*, Raphael the angel gives magical directions for driving away the devil by taking a fish's liver, burning it, and causing a magical smoke (6:6).
- The book of *Tobit* says Raphael the angel accepted prayers offered to him (12:12), which angels never accept in Scripture (Rev. 22:8-9).

## Jesus and the Apostles Never Quoted Them

The second reason why we don't accept the apocrypha is that *Jesus and the apostles never quoted them*. We have a saying that goes

---

7. Cf. Turretin, *Institutes*, 1:103-04.

something like this: his silence was deafening. What that means is that when you listen to someone speak on a subject, you can tell what they believe not only by what they say but by what they don't say. If I'm a politician who wants to run for the Republican Party, and I give a speech about why you should vote for me as a conservative candidate, but I never talk about Abraham Lincoln or Ronald Reagan, you can tell how conservative I really am. The same is true if I run as a Democrat but never mention FDR, JFK, or Barack Obama.

So again, in Luke 24, we read of Jesus' explaining to His disciples only from the law, the prophets, and the psalms that He was the Messiah who was to die and rise again. His silence about the apocryphal books is deafening. Even more, I challenge you to read through the New Testament and write a list of every time Jesus and the apostles quote other writings. They quote from the Old Testament (the apostles cite pagan poets and philosophers a couple of times in their witnessing to them). Again, when it comes to the apocrypha, the silence is deafening.

## The Ancient Church Never Received Them

Finally, let me give you a historical reason for why we don't accept the apocryphal books: *the ancient Church never received them*. Let me say that I've read the Church fathers looking for their approval of the apocryphal books. I've read Roman Catholic authors especially, giving their reasons for including them in the canon and I've read Protestant responses. Here's what's clear: historic Protestants are the true catholics because the ancient Church recognized no other books than what we have. Yes, every once in a while, a writer quotes an apocryphal text or even lists a book in their list of canonical books that we don't have in our canon. *This is the exception.* When one Church council received one non-canonical book and another council received another, the one thing that remained common among them both was the list of books we accept. For example, Melito of Sardis in A.D. 170 listed our Old Testament canon.[8] The Synod of Laodicea in the mid-fourth century said no 'uncanonical

---

8. Eusebius, *Church History* 4:26, trans. Arthur Cushman McGiffert, *Nicene and Post-Nicene Fathers: Second Series*, ed. Philip Schaff and Henry Wace, 14 vols. (1890; repr, Peabody, MA: Hendrickson Publishers, fourth printing 2004), 206 col. 1-2.

books may be read in the church, but only canonical books of the Old and New Testaments.'[9]

Athanasius, the great defender of the Trinitarian faith, listed the Scriptures of our Bible and then said: 'These are the fountains of salvation, that he who thirsts may be satisfied with the living words they contain. In these alone the teaching of godliness is proclaimed. Let no one add to these; let nothing be taken away from them.' Augustine wrote to Jerome (*ca.* 342/347–420) saying:

> For I confess to your Charity that I have learned to yield this respect and honour only to the canonical books of Scripture: of these alone do I most firmly believe that the authors were completely free from error. And if in these writings I am perplexed by anything which appears to me opposed to truth, I do not hesitate to suppose that either the manuscript is faulty, or the translator has not caught the meaning of what was said, or I myself have failed to understand it. As to all other writings, in reading them, however great the superiority of the authors to myself in sanctity and learning, I do not accept their teaching as true on the mere ground of the opinion being held by them; but only because they have succeeded in convincing my judgment of its truth either by means of these canonical writings themselves, or by arguments addressed to my reason.[10]

The reason these books were called 'apocryphal' was that their origin and authorship were unknown, or hidden. In fact, the ancient fathers Epiphanius (310/320–403) and Augustine said 'apocryphal' meant that they were removed from a hidden crypt, while Jerome and Rufinus of Aquileia (344/45–411) said this meant their authority was hidden. So much for the fathers being on Rome's side.

Further, the Church fathers belabor this point, that there is a distinction between what they called the canon of faith and the canon of ecclesiastical reading.[11] What they meant was that the

9.    Canon LVIII, 'Synod of Laodicea A.D. 343–381,' in *Nicene and Post-Nicene Fathers: Second Series,* ed. Philip Schaff and Henry Wace, 14 vols. (1900; repr, Peabody, MA: Hendrickson Publishers, fourth printing 2004), 14:158.

10.    Augustine, *Letter 82 in Nicene and Post-Nicene Fathers: First Series,* ed. Philip Schaff, 14 vols. (1886; repr, Peabody, MA: Hendrickson Publishers, fourth printing 2004), 1:350 col. 2.

11.    Jerome, 'Preface to Proverbs, Ecclesiastes, and the Song of Songs,' in *Post-Nicene Fathers: Second Series,* ed. Philip Schaff and Henry Wace, 14 vols. (1893;

71

books in our Old and New Testaments alone were read to prove points of doctrine, while other books were permitted to be read for moral inspiration but not for doctrinal instruction.[12] As Protestants, we're distinctly catholic on this point. Our protest isn't against the catholic Church but with the Roman Catholic Church in particular. For example, the 1561 Belgic Confession says:

'We distinguish between these holy books and the apocryphal ones...The church may certainly read these books and learn from them as far as they agree with the canonical books. But they do not have such power and virtue that one could confirm from their testimony any point of faith or of the Christian religion. Much less can they detract from the authority of the other holy books.' The 1571 *Thirty-Nine Articles of Religion* of the Reformed English Church contrast the canonical books of Holy Scripture from the apocryphal:

> In the name of the holy Scripture we do understand those Canonical Books of the Old and New Testament, of whose authority was never any doubt in the Church. And the other Books (as Hierome [Jerome] saith) the Church doth read for example of life and instruction of manners; but yet doth not apply them to establish any doctrine.... All the Books of the New Testament, as they are commonly received, we do receive, and account them Canonical (art. 6).[13]

This is completely consistent with the medieval commentary on Scripture called the *Glossa Ordinaria*. Its 1498 prologue says:

> Many people, who do not give much attention to the holy scriptures, think that all the books contained in the Bible

---

repr, Peabody, MA: Hendrickson Publishers, fourth printing 2004), 6:492 col. 1-2; Augustine, 'Reply to Faustus the Manichaean' 11.5 in *Post-Nicene Fathers: First Series*, ed. Philip Schaff, 14 vols. (1887; repr, Peabody, MA: Hendrickson Publishers, fourth printing 2004), 4:180 col. 1-2.

12. 'Prologue' to the *Glossa Ordinaria* (1498) cited in William Webster, *The Old Testament Canon and the Apocrypha: A Survey of the History of the Apocrypha from the Jewish Age to the Reformation* (Battle Ground, WA: Christian Resources, 2002), 60-61.

13. The *Thirty-Nine Articles* list the following as non-canonical: 3–4 Esdras, Baruch the Prophet, the Song of the Three Children, Tobias, Judith, the rest of the Book of Esther, the Book of Wisdom, Jesus the Son of Sirach, Susanna, Bel and the Dragon, the Prayer of Manasses, and 1–2 Maccabees (*Reformed Confessions of the 16th and 17th Centuries in English Translation: Volume 2, 1552–1566*, ed. James T. Dennison, Jr. [Grand Rapids: Reformation Heritage Books, 2010], 755-56.

should be honored and adored with equal veneration, not knowing how to distinguish among the canonical and non-canonical books, the latter of which the Jews number among the apocrypha.[14]

At that time, it was customary to include in copies of the Bible the Old Testament, Apocrypha, and New Testament. The important point from the perspective of the Glossa is that it rejects equating the canon with the apocrypha. The distinction between canonical and non-canonical is explained: 'The canonical books have been brought about through the dictation of the Holy Spirit. It is not known, however, at which time or by which authors the non-canonical or apocryphal books were produced.'[15] In fact, one of Martin Luther's great opponents, Cardinal Cajetan (1469–1534), encouraged his readers not to be 'disturbed...if thou should find any where, either in the sacred councils of the sacred doctors, these [apocryphal] books reckoned as canonical.' Why did he say this? He cited Jerome's distinction between the canon and apocrypha, between the rule for confirming matters of faith versus the rule for edification of the saints. [footnote: Cited in Whitaker, *Disputation*, 48,]

With this distinction in mind, we can see where the Reformers received the non-canonical books in a limited way: 'Since, nevertheless, they are very good and useful, and nothing is found in them which contradicts the canonical books, the church reads them and permits them to be read by the faithful for devotion and edification.' Again, in what sounds completely contradictory to Trent but consistent with Reformed catholicism, they say:

> Their authority, however, is not considered adequate for proving those things which come into doubt or contention, or for confirming the authority of ecclesiastical dogma.... But the canonical books are of such authority that whatever is contained therein is held to be true firmly and indisputably, and likewise that which is clearly demonstrated from them.

---

14. Cited in William Webster, *The Old Testament Canon and the Apocrypha* (Christian Resources, 2003), 60.

15. Cited in Webster, *The Old Testament Canon and the Apocrypha*, 61.

## Conclusion

Let me conclude by noting again that Rome decreed on April 8, 1546 at the Council of Trent that those who don't receive the Old Testament, New Testament, *and* the apocryphal books in the Vulgate translation of the Bible, *and* Rome's many traditions are *anathema* – condemned. After all we've seen in this chapter, I trust you can see that Rome condemned the prophets, the apostles, the ancient Church, the medieval Church, and most importantly, Jesus Himself! I'll take my chances with Jesus. He's the confidence I need.

# Chapter 7 SUFFICIENCY

## *Complete, Equipped for Every Good Work*

> But as for you, continue in what you have learned and have firmly believed, knowing from whom you learned it and how from childhood you have been acquainted with the sacred writings, which are able to make you wise for salvation through faith in Christ Jesus. All Scripture is breathed out by God and profitable for teaching, for reproof, for correction, and for training in righteousness, that the man of God may be complete, equipped for every good work (2 Tim. 3:14-17).

When it comes to what you believe and how you live as a Christian, is the Bible enough? I'm not asking whether the Bible says everything about everything (a false view of sufficiency),[1] but whether in what it says about faith and godliness, theology and piety, it says what you need to know. This is the question of the sufficiency of Scripture.[2] At the time of the Reformation in England when there was societal ignorance of the Scriptures and a lack of pastors to teach the Word, a set of 'homilies' (sermons) were written to be read from pulpits. The first opens with this line: 'Unto a Christian man there can be

---

1. See T. David Gordon, 'The Insufficiency of Scripture,' *Modern Reformation* 11:1 (January/February 2002): 18-23.

2. On the sufficiency of Scripture, see Noel Weeks, *The Sufficiency of Scripture* (Edinburgh: The Banner of Truth Trust, 1988).

nothing either more necessary or profitable that [sic] the knowledge of Holy Scripture, forasmuch as in it is contained God's true Word, setting forth his glory and also man's duty.'[3]

This question is still relevant in our distinction from the Roman and Orthodox Churches and their rejection of the sufficiency of Scripture. As we saw, in 1546 Rome said it 'received and venerates with a feeling of piety and reverence all the books both of the Old and New Testaments… also the traditions…'[4] This led John Calvin to reply: 'By one article they have obtained the means of proving what they please out of Scripture, and escaping from every passage that might be urged against them.'[5] In other words, when you claim Scripture is not sufficient but you need tradition, you can say what you want about faith and life and you can defend yourself from every criticism found in the Scripture. More recently, in 1965, Pope Paul VI declared: 'It is not from Sacred Scripture alone that the Church draws her certainty about everything which has been revealed. Therefore both sacred tradition and Sacred Scripture are to be accepted and venerated with the same sense of loyalty and reverence.'[6]

This issue is important because it brings up whether you can pick up a Bible, read it, and know what God requires to be saved from sin and to live to His glory. In the words of Augustine: 'In clearly expressed passages of scripture one can find all the things that concern faith and the moral life (namely hope and love).'[7] Do we need something else, which Rome describes as its parallel traditions or which Orthodoxy calls 'the Tradition'? Yet the biblical commentator Theodoret of Cyrus (393–458/466), whom some members of the Assyrian Church of the East and Eastern Orthodox

---

3.   'A Fruitful Exhortation to the Reading and Knowledge of Holy Scripture,' in *The Books of Homilies*, 7.

4.   *Canons and Decrees of the Council of Trent*, trans. Schroeder, 17.

5.   Calvin, 'Acts of the Council of Trent with the Antidote,' *Selected Works*, 3:69.

6.   *Dei Verbum*, 2.9. As found at http://www.vatican.va/archive/hist_councils/ii_vatican_council/documents/vat-ii_const_19651118_dei-verbum_en.html (Accessed January 22, 2021). See also *Catechism of the Catholic Church* 82 (New York: Doubleday 1995), 31.

7.   Saint Augustine, *On Christian Teaching*, trans. R. P. H. Green, Oxford Worlds Classics (1997; repr., Oxford: Oxford University Press, 1999), 2.31

Churches consider a saint, said 'not to introduce anything into holy Scripture but to be content with the teaching of the Spirit.'[8]

Our earliest extant and complete defense of the early Christians, the *Apology* of Aristides of Athens (*ca.* A.D. 125), addressed Emperor Hadrian (76–138) on how he could confirm the teachings advocated in the *Apology*. Where did Aristides instruct Hadrian to go? To their [Christian] 'writings'; he didn't appeal to the Pope or Tradition. Indeed, this is how Aristides himself came to his knowledge of the Christian faith and possession of its truth for himself:

> But the Christians, O King, while they went about and made search, have found the truth; and *as we learned from their writings*, they have come nearer to truth and genuine knowledge than the rest of the nations.[9]

Hadrian, too, could take up these writings and learn:

> And as for their words and their precepts, O King, and their glorying in their worship, and the hope of earning according to the work of each one of them their recompense which they look for in another world, *you may learn about these from their writings.*... For great indeed, and wonderful is their doctrine to him who will search into it and reflect upon it.... *Take, then, their writings, and read therein, and lo! you will find that I have not put forth these things on my own authority, nor spoken thus as their advocate; but since I read in their writings I was fully assured of these things as also of things which are to come.*[10]

In this brief section, Aristides repeats three times that 'their writings' are the source (the only source he mentions, in fact) for Christian dogma. He's careful to distinguish their authority from his own, which he doesn't claim to have. The authority of his words is simply the authority of truth, which Hadrian is exhorted to verify for himself. He doesn't even feel the need to be their 'advocate'; in the last analysis, the writings need no advocate. On the contrary, they

---

8.    Theodoret of Cyrus, *Questions on the Octateuch: Volume 2,* trans. Robert C. Hill, Library of Early Christianity (Washington, D.C.: Catholic University of America Press, 2007), 25.

9.    *The Apology of Aristides the Philosopher* 15, trans. D. M. Kay in *Ante-Nicene Fathers,* ed. Allan Menzies, 10 vols. (1896; repr, Peabody, MA: Hendrickson Publishers, fourth printing 2004), 9:276, col. 2.

10.    Ibid., 16, 9:278 col. 2.

serve as *his* advocate or helper: they give Aristides 'full assurance' of the 'things which are to come.' Aristides only 'declares.' He serves as witness to the Witness whence Christian teachings come with divine authority. Aristides' words are an indication, pointing his readers back to the law and the testimony (Isa. 8:20), where we find the divine address and summons of the Triune God.

What do we mean when we say the Scriptures are 'sufficient'? Again, we are not saying that the Scriptures say everything about everything, so that we only read the Bible as Christians. The sufficiency of Scripture correctly understood means that the things we need to know for salvation and godliness are revealed by God in His Word:

> The whole counsel of God concerning all things necessary for his own glory, man's salvation, faith and life, is either expressly set down in Scripture, or by good and necessary consequence may be deduced from Scripture: unto which nothing at any time is to be added, whether by new revelations of the Spirit, or traditions of men (WCF 1.6).

The question of the Bible being enough or sufficient is answered in 2 Timothy 3:14-17. We'll note the connection between the Scriptures being breathed out by God, meaning that He spoke them, and the result being that they are 'able to make you wise for salvation' and are 'profitable for…training in righteousness.'

### Sufficient for Salvation

The Scriptures are 'sufficient for salvation.' As Paul exhorts Timothy, 'continue in what you have learned and have firmly believed' (v. 14). What did he learn and believe? 'The sacred writings' (v. 15). His grandmother Lois and mother Eunice (1:4) taught him these from childhood. Notice what Paul specifically reminds Timothy of concerning these writings: *which are able to make you wise for salvation through faith in Christ Jesus* (v. 15). The Scriptures are sufficient for salvation. Focus on the word *able*. Paul does not say the Scriptures *can* make you wise for salvation as if it were a hypothetical. He uses a familiar Greek verb that denotes ability and capacity, *dunamai*.[11]

---

11.   'δύναμαι.' Bauer, Arndt, Gingrich, and Danker, *Greek-English Lexicon*, 207 col. 1.

It's related to the familiar noun for power and might, *dunamis*.[12] The sacred writings of the Old and New Testaments have the power and the might to grant to you wisdom from above so that you will know God's saving grace. How? Because they're sacred or holy (v. 15) and breathed out (v. 16). They're the very voice of God. The ancient father Chrysostom said on 2 Timothy 3:16-17 that Paul had 'offered much exhortation and consolation from other sources' but then 'adds that which is more perfect, derived from the Scriptures.' Of their sufficiency he said:

> For thence we shall know, whether we ought to learn or to be ignorant of anything. And thence we may disprove what is false, thence we may be corrected and brought to a right mind, may be comforted and consoled, and if anything is deficient, we may have it added to us...without [Scripture] therefore he cannot be perfect. Thou hast the Scriptures, he says, in place of me. If thou wouldest learn anything, thou mayest learn it from them. And if he thus wrote to Timothy, who was filled with the Spirit, how much more to us![13]

The *Thirty-Nine Articles* say: 'Holy Scripture containeth all things necessary to salvation: so that whatsoever is not read therein, nor may be proved thereby, is not to be required of any man, that it should be believed an article of the Faith, or be thought requisite or necessary to salvation' (art. 6).[14] 'This is why theologians like Johannes Maccovius (1588–1644) concluded: 'Scripture is perfect... because it expresses those things in so far as they are necessary for us to know in order to be saved.'[15]

It's as easy as this: if I told you that the author of your favorite book was available to talk to you at Barnes & Noble, would you get in line to talk with him or her, or would you go find the first store employee and ask them about the book? The Bible *is* the Word of

---

12. 'δύναμις.' Bauer, Arndt, Gingrich, and Danker, *Greek-English Lexicon*, 207 col. 1-208 col. 1.

13. Chrysostom, *Homilies on the Second Epistle of St. Paul the Apostle to Timothy*, in *Nicene and Post-Nicene Fathers: First Series*, ed. Philip Schaff, 14 volumes (1889; repr., Peabody, MA: Hendrickson Publishers, fourth printing 2004), 13:509 col. 1-510 col. 1.

14. *Reformed Confessions of the 16th and 17th Centuries in English Translation: Volume 2, 1552–1566*, ed. James T. Dennison, Jr. (Grand Rapids: Reformation Heritage Books, 2010), 755.

15. Maccovius, *Scholastic Discourse*, 65.

God, His living and active voice to us. We can hear directly from the author of salvation about salvation.

Why is this important for us? Rome says that alongside Scripture is equally authoritative tradition. Orthodoxy says their faithful passing down of the Tradition is sacred. Timothy did receive the faithful passing down of the sacred writings – a holy tradition; there's no doubting that. But note even more, that Paul only attributes to the Scriptures the ability to grant heavenly wisdom for a saving knowledge of God. He doesn't attribute this authority to any man or group of men. In the words of the Church of England's first homily again: 'There is no truth nor doctrine necessary for our justification and everlasting salvation but that is, or may be, drawn out of that foundation and well of truth.'[16]

## Sufficient for Doctrine

Relatedly, the Scriptures are *sufficient for doctrine*. Paul goes on to say that all Scripture is breathed out by God and profitable for *teaching* (v. 16), which the old King James translated as *doctrine*.[17] *Didaskalia* is the content (teaching) of what a teacher teaches; hence doctrine or even theology. What we need for our 'theology,' which Augustine defined as 'an account or explanation of the divine nature,' is found in the Word.[18] I'm no engineer or architect, but think about a blueprint. An engineer has an idea for a building in his mind, which he then reveals upon a blueprint. All he envisions in his mind is upon that blueprint. Then a builder takes the blueprint and executes the plan in reality. The Word of God reveals the mind of God concerning all that is necessary for us to know about God, His world, and ourselves. We, like a builder, can turn to them to try as faithfully as possible to implement God's will in our doctrine, our creeds, and our confessional statements.

Commenting on Jesus' words about 'enter[ing]...by the door' (John 10:1), Theophylact (d. *ca.* 1107), the medieval Orthodox archbishop of Ochrid and Bulgaria, interpreted 'the door' as the Scriptures. He explained their importance: 'The Scriptures are indeed a door leading to God: they deny entry to wolves and heretics;

16. 'A Fruitful Exhortation to the Reading and Knowledge of Holy Scripture,' in *The Books of Homilies*, 7.

17. 'διδασκαλία.' Bauer, Arndt, Gingrich, and Danker, *Greek-English Lexicon*, 191 col. 2.

18. *de divinitate rationem sive sermonem*. Augustine, *The City of God*, 8.1.

they keep us safe; they communicate whatever good thing we may desire to learn.' Scripture, not tradition, speaks to us from God about whatever we desire to learn: 'the Lord is also rebuking the scribes, who disregarded the law God gave to Moses and replaced it with man-made ordinances and traditions.'[19]

### 'But What About Tradition?'

The Roman and Orthodox objection is this: 'but doesn't Paul also say we are to "hold to the traditions"?' (2 Thess. 2:15).[20] Yes, he does; but 2 Thessalonians is not in contrast to 2 Timothy. The 'traditions' of which Paul speaks are not *extra* – outside the Scriptures. They're not co-authoritative truths passed down *in addition to* Scripture, but the passing down of the teaching of the apostles in one of two ways: preaching and writing. Paul preached and Paul wrote. He didn't write everything he preached, but he reminded his people in his writings of his preaching and even summarized for them the main points of truth. As Calvin responded to Rome, the apostles handed down tradition that they didn't write, but this had nothing to do with essential doctrines but only with external rites to keep the Church in order.[21]

The serious misunderstanding that we are to believe and obey things in addition to the truths in Scripture is analogous to the Israelites' misunderstanding. The Lord gave them His Word through the patriarchs, prophets, and poets, which were later written in the Old Testament Scriptures. Yet, their teachers heaped up a whole host of unwritten traditions in addition to what was written. What was the Lord's attitude towards these traditions? At the end of the time of Moses, the Lord renewed this covenant with His people. He said to them, 'You shall not add to the word that I command you, nor take from it, that you may keep the commandments of the LORD your God that I command you' (Deut. 4:2). While prescribing

---

19. Theophylact, *The Explanation of the Holy Gospel According to John,* trans. Fr. Christopher Stade, Blessed Theophylact's Explanation of the New Testament 4 (Chrysostom Press, 2007), 164. Interestingly, the sixteenth-century English theologian, John Jewel, cited this passage of Theophylact. 'A Treatise of the Holy Scriptures,' *Works* 4:1170.

20. For an academic discussion of tradition in the history of the Church, see Heiko Oberman, *Forerunners of the Reformation: The Shape of Late Medieval Thought Illustrated by Key Documents,* trans, Paul L. Nyhus (NY: Holt, Rinehart and Winston, 1966), 53-66.

21. Calvin, *Acts of the Council of Trent with the Antidote,* 70.

the future place of worship and warning His people not to worship another god, He said: 'Everything that I command you, you shall be careful to do. You shall not add to it or take from it' (Deut. 12:32). There was even a proverb among the Israelites: 'Every word of God proves true; he is a shield to those who take refuge in him. Do not add to his words, lest he rebuke you and you be found a liar' (Prov. 30:5-6). Israel was to be governed not by their cultural or even religious traditions, but by the Word of the Lord. As He told them during their wilderness journey, 'man does not live by bread alone, but man lives by every word that comes from the mouth of the LORD' (Deut. 8:3). In the time of the prophets, the Lord said: 'To the teaching and to the testimony! If they will not speak according to this word it is because they have no dawn,' meaning, they have no light, no enlightenment from the Lord Himself (Isa. 8:20). The Lord went on to say: 'This people draw near with their mouth and honor me with their lips, while their hearts are far from me, and their fear of me is a commandment taught by men' (Isa. 29:13). In the time of our Lord Jesus' ministry, He said of these teachers of traditions that they were 'blind guides' (Matt. 15:14). Finally, in the apostolic age, Paul told the Corinthians that he wanted them to 'learn by us not to go beyond what is written' (1 Cor. 4:6). Consider this: the 'tradition' Paul spoke of didn't go beyond his writings. When it comes to doctrine, we are ever to remember the prohibition of both the Old and New Testaments, that we are not to add to or take from the Word of God (Deut. 4:2; Gal. 1:8; Rev. 22:18-19). Over time, this principle has proven to be true: '...he who today places something else on a par with the Bible is practically certain to exalt that other thing above the Bible tomorrow.'[22]

One way to see our positive view of tradition is by considering the role of the Church fathers. According to John Jewel (1522–1571):

> They be interpreters of the word of God. They were learned men, and learned fathers; the instruments of the mercy of God, and vessels full of grace. We despise them not, we read them, we reverence them, and give thanks unto God for them. They were witnesses unto the truth, they were worthy pillars and ornaments in the church of God. Yet may they not be compared with the word of God. We may

---

22.   R. B. Kuiper, *The Bible Tells Us So* (1968, repr, Edinburgh: The Banner of Truth, 1978), 22.

> not build upon them: we may not make them the foundation
> and warrant of our conscience: we may not put our trust in
> them. Our trust is in the name of the Lord.[23]

Similarly, various fathers spoke of their role. In speaking of interpreting Scripture, Origen (184–253) said it succinctly and self-deprecatingly: 'it is necessary to take the Scriptures as *witnesses*. For without witnesses, our interpretations and exegeses are unfaithful.'[24] Augustine said it briefly as well: 'Notice the words, *Says the Lord*; it does not say: "Says Donatus," or "Rogatus," or "Vincent," or "Hilary," or "Ambrose," or "Augustine," but, *Says the Lord*.'[25] He said it a little more lengthily:

> ...we ought not to regard the writings of any people, though
> Catholic and highly praised, as being on par with the
> canonical scriptures, so that we are not permitted – always
> preserving the respect owed to those men – to criticize and
> reject something in their writings if we should perhaps find
> something that they held other than is found in the truth,
> when understood with the help of God by ourselves or by
> others. That is the way I am with the writings of others; that
> is the way I want my readers to be.[26]

So what about the sufficiency of Scripture for doctrine in relation to Christian tradition? Carl Trueman nicely explains: '...*tradition* is not the issue; it is how one defines that tradition, and how one understands the way it connects to Scripture...this was the crux of the Reformation, which was not so much a struggle between Scripture and tradition as between different types of tradition.'[27]

---

23. Jewel, 'A Treatise of the Holy Scriptures,' *Works* 4:1173.

24. Origen, *Homilies on Jeremiah and Homily on 1 Kings 28,* trans. John Clark Smith, The Fathers of the Church: A New Translation (Washington, D.C.: The Catholic University of America Press, 1998), 9. Also cited in Jewel, 'A Treatise of the Holy Scriptures,' *Works* 4:1173.

25. Augustine, *Letters* 1–99, trans. Roland Teske, The Works of Saint Augustine: A Translation for the 21st Century II/1 (Hyde Park/New York: New City Press, 2001), 93.6.20. Also cited in Jewel, 'A Treatise of the Holy Scriptures,' *Works* 4:1173.

26. Augustine, *Letters* 100–155, trans. Roland Teske, The Works of Saint Augustine: A Translation for the 21st Century II/2 (Hyde Park/New York: New City Press, 2003), 148.5.15. Also cited in Jewel, 'A Treatise of the Holy Scriptures,' *Works* 4:1173.

27. Carl Trueman, *The Creedal Imperative* (Wheaton: Crossway, 2012), 11.

## Sufficient for Godliness

Because the Scriptures are sufficient for how we are to be saved and for what we are to believe concerning God, they are also *sufficient for godliness*. In Paul's language, not only is 'all Scripture breathed out by God but it is also profitable…for reproof, for correction, and for training in righteousness, that the man of God may be complete, equipped for every good work' (vv. 16-17). The English Puritan, William Ames (1576–1633), said: 'All things necessary to salvation are contained in the Scriptures and also those things necessary for the instruction and edification of the church.'[28] Paul's words that our godliness finds direction in the Scripture leads us to the necessary application that his words stand against all the man-made traditions especially of the Roman Church. In addition to Paul's words, concerning how we are to live the Christian life the Church fathers say similarly. Jerome said, 'That which does not have authority from the Scriptures, we can as easily despise as approve,'[29] and, 'The sword of God smites whatever they draw and forges from a pretended apostolic tradition, without the authority and testimony of the Scriptures.'[30] Basil of Caesarea (330–379) said: 'It is a proof of unbelief and a sign of pride either to weaken any of those things which are written or to introduce what is not written.'[31]

## Conclusion: A Sure Refuge

In conclusion, all this means we have a sure refuge in the God who sufficiently revealed Himself in the Scriptures for what it means to be a Christian. What are we to believe about God? Look to the Scriptures. How are we to live before the face of God? Look to the Scriptures. There was an ancient commentary on the Gospel of Matthew that was never completed, the so-called *Opus Imperfectum*, 'the imperfect work.' In its comments on Jesus' teaching concerning the last days in Matthew 24, we read this:

> There can be no trial of true Christianity; and Christians, which desire to know the truth, whereupon they may build their faith, have no other refuge, but to try and learn this

---

28.    William Ames, *The Marrow of Theology*, trans. John Dykstra Eusden (1968; repr., Grand Rapids: Baker Books, second printing 1997), 187.

29.    Cited in Turretin, *Institutes*, 1:139.

30.    Ibid., 1.143

31.    Ibid., 1:139.

by the scriptures. For...heretics have the counterfeit and likeness of those things which are proper to Christ. They have churches, they have the scriptures of God, they have baptism, they have the Lord's supper, and all other things like the true church; yea, they have Christ himself. He therefore that will know which is the true church of Christ, how may he know it but by the scriptures? Therefore our Lord, knowing that there should be such confusion of things in the latter days, commandeth that Christians which live in the profession of christian faith, and are desirous to settle themselves upon a sure ground of faith, should go to no other thing but to the scriptures.[32]

Because you have this sure refuge for doctrine and doxology, theology and piety, immerse yourself in the Word. Doing so is like traveling on the king's narrow but straight highway. In the words of J.C. Ryle, 'Departing from this principle we enter on a pathless wilderness.'[33]

---

32.  Jewel, 'A Treatise of the Holy Scriptures,' *Works* 4:1170.

33.  J.C. Ryle, *Expository Thoughts on the Gospels: Luke 1–10* (Grand Rapids: Baker Book House, reprinted 2007), 371.

# Chapter 8   PERSPICUITY
## *Open My Eyes That I May Behold*

'Open my eyes, that I may behold wondrous things out of
your law' *(*Ps. 119:18).

Can you pick up your Bible, begin reading at Genesis 1, complete
the entire tome, and then be able to summarize its basic message
about God, humanity, how God saves, and how you're to live? There
was a time when the Roman Catholic Church forbade its members
from even trying. Roman Popes, Councils, and Kings forbade the
translation of the Scriptures into the language of the people. For
example, from the time of St. Methodius (815–885), monks were
permitted to use their own language, Old Church Slavonic. Yet
after his death in 920, Pope John X (d. 928) forbade Old Church
Slavonic, the Lateran Synod of 1059 upheld this, and Popes Nicholas
II (990/995–1061) and Alexander II (1010/1015–1073) confirmed
this. In a 1080 letter to King Vratislav II of Bohemia (1032–1092),
Pope Gregory VII explained his predecessors' revoking permission
for the Slavs to use their own language:

> Since your excellency has asked that we would allow the
> divine office to be said among you in Slavonic, know that
> we can by no means favourably answer this your petition.
> For it is clear to those who reflect often upon it, that not
> without reason has it pleased Almighty God that holy

scripture should be a secret in certain places, lest, if it were plainly apparent to all men, perchance it would be little esteemed and be subject to disrespect; or it might be falsely understood by those of mediocre learning, and lead to error. Nor does it avail as an excuse that certain religious men have patiently suffered the simple folk who asked for it, or have sent them away uncorrected, which, after Christianity had grown stronger, and when religion was increasing, were corrected by subtle examination. Wherefore we forbid what you have so imprudently demanded of the authority of St Peter, and we command you to resist this vain rashness with all your might, to the honour of Almighty God.[1]

According to the self-proclaimed representative of Christ on earth–the Pope, it pleased God to keep Scripture secret so that it would not be treated irreverently and disrespectfully or be misunderstood and lead to error.

Pope Innocent III (1160/61–1216) later wrote to the bishop of Metz in 1199: 'The secret mysteries of the faith ought not to be explained to all men in all places, since they cannot be everywhere understood by all men; but only to those who can conceive them with a faithful mind.'[2] Why? 'For such is the depth of divine scripture, that not only the simple and illiterate, but even the prudent and learned, are not fully sufficient to try to understand it.'[3] He illustrated from the story of Israel at Mount Sinai being warned not to come close and touch the mountain 'lest, apparently, any simple and unlearned person should presume to attain to the sublimity of holy scripture.'[4] Yet, the result of such thinking is that God revealed (made Himself known) Himself more in darkness than in creation! In the following year he sent a representative to order the burning of French Bible translations and in 1202 his envoy, Bishop Guido of Präneste, enforced several provisions in Leuven including that all books in Latin and German dealing with Holy Scripture were to be delivered to the bishop.

---

1.   Margaret Deanesley, *The Lollard Bible and Other Medieval Biblical Versions* (Cambridge: Cambridge University Press, 1920), 24.

2.   Deanesley, *The Lollard Bible*, 31.

3.   Deanesley, *The Lollard Bible*, 31.

4.   Deanesley, *The Lollard Bible*, 31.

In 1229 the Council of Toulouse announced a Bible ban for lay people in their province, except for the Psalter and Breviary in Latin:

> We prohibit also that the laity should be permitted to have the books of the Old and New Testaments; unless anyone from the motives of devotion should wish to have the Psalter or the Breviary for divine offices or the hours of the blessed Virgin; but we most strictly forbid their having any translation of these books.'[5]

The Roman Church only allowed *its* devotional material and not the source from which they came. One wonders why? In the words of Margaret Deanesley, 'the attitude of the mediaeval Church to biblical translations has thus been seen to have been one of toleration in principle, and distrust in practice.'[6]

Finally, at the aforementioned Council of Trent in 1564, 'Ten Rules Concerning Prohibited Books' were approved by Pope Pius IV.' Rule 4 said:

> Since it is clear from experience that if the Sacred Books are permitted everywhere and without discrimination in the vernacular, there will by reason of the boldness of men arise therefrom more harm than good, the matter is in this respect left to the judgment of the bishop or inquisitor, who may with the advice of the pastor or confessor permit the reading of the Sacred Books translated into the vernacular by Catholic authors to those who they know will derive from such reading no harm but rather an increase of faith and piety, which permission they must have in writing. Those, however, who presume to read or possess them without such permission may not receive absolution from their sins till they have handed them over to the ordinary. Bookdealers who sell or in any other way supply Bibles written in the vernacular to anyone who has not this permission, shall lose the price of the books, which is to be applied by the bishop to pious purposes, and in keeping with the nature of the crime they shall be subject to other penalties which are left to the judgment of the same bishop. Regulars who have not

---

5. *Heresy and Authority in Medieval Europe: Documents in Translation*, ed. Edward Peters (London: Scholar Press, 1980), 195.

6. Deanesley, *The Lollard Bibles*, 372.

the permission of their superiors may not read or purchase them.[7]

Several nineteenth-century Popes continued this attack on Bible distribution and lay reading. Pope Pius VII (1742–1823) denounced the Bible Society's circulation of the Scriptures: 'It is evidence from experience, that the holy Scriptures, when circulated in the vulgar tongue [common language], have, through the temerity of men, produced more harm than benefit.'[8] Pope Leo XII (1760–1829) called the Protestant Bible the 'Gospel of the Devil' in an encyclical letter of 1824. Pope Gregory XVI (1765–1846) railed 'against the publication, distribution, reading, and possession of books of the holy Scriptures translated into the vulgar tongue'[9] [common language].

Thankfully, Rome has changed. I say this as genuine praise. At the same time, it's yet another evidence that the popular myth so many evangelicals fall pray to is false: Rome never changes. In 1943, Pope Pius XII issued the encyclical called Divino Afflante Spiritu, 'inspired by the Divine Spirit,' in which he said this to the laity:

> The same veneration the Bishops should endeavor daily to increase and perfect among the faithful committed to their care, encouraging all those initiatives by which men, filled with apostolic zeal, laudably strive to excite and foster among Catholics a greater knowledge of and love for the Sacred Books. Let them favor therefore and lend help to those pious associations whose aim it is to spread copies of the Sacred Letters, especially of the Gospels, among the faithful, and to procure by every means that in Christian families the same be read daily with piety and devotion; let them efficaciously recommend by word and example, whenever the liturgical laws permit, the Sacred Scriptures translated, with the approval of the Ecclesiastical authority, into modern languages...[10]

---

7. *Canons and Decrees of the Council of Trent*, trans. Schroeder, 274-75.

8. *The Papal Controversy Involving the Claim of the Roman Catholic Church to be the Church of God* (St. Louis: National Baptist Publication Co., 1892), 477.

9. *The Papal Controversy*, 482.

10. As found at http://www.vatican.va/content/pius-xii/en/encyclicals/documents/hf_p-xii_enc_30091943_divino-afflante-spiritu.html (Accessed January 13, 2021). See also *Dei Verbum*, 6.22, 25. As found at http://www.vatican.va/archive/

That's quite a change! Now, in its Catechism, Rome 'forcefully and specifically exhorts all the Christian faithful...to learn the surpassing knowledge of Jesus Christ, by frequent reading of the divine Scriptures.'[11] Of course, this proves the point that 'all synods or councils, since the Apostles' times, whether general or particular, may err; and many have erred' (Westminster Confession, 31.4).[12] Rome isn't infallible; Orthodoxy isn't infallible; Protestantism isn't infallible. Only God and His Word are. But even now, Rome still insists that the Pope, the teachers of the Church, the Church's council's, the Church fathers, and the list goes on, are necessary to understand the Word.

In relation to the previous chapter on sufficiency is 'perspicuity.'[13] In other words, is the Bible clear when you read it? In what ways? In what ways is it not? I want you to be assured of your answer to this question. *The Bible is clear (perspicuous) in matters relating to salvation and godliness.*

## What the Clarity of Scripture Is Not

The typical Roman or Orthodox response to us saying that 'the Bible is clear' is to say we believe every layperson can pick up a copy of the Bible and understand everything. As one popular Roman Catholic blog writer said, '...the typical Protestant view is that Scripture is so clear that there are no ambiguities needing authoritative interpretation by the Church. As classically articulated, this doctrine holds anyone guided by the Holy Spirit can come to

---

hist_councils/ii_vatican_council/documents/vat-ii_const_19651118_dei-verbum_en.html (Accessed January 22, 2021).

11.   *Catechism of the Catholic Church*, 133, p. 43.

12.   Reformed Confessions: Volume 4, 270. See also Belgic Confession, art. 7: 'Therefore we must not consider human writings – no matter how holy their authors may have been – equal to the divine writings; nor may we put custom, nor the majority, nor age, nor the passage of time or persons, nor councils, decrees, or official decisions above the truth of God.... For all human beings are liars by nature and more vain than vanity itself.' The Thirty-Nine Articles, art. 21, also says, '...when [General Councils] be gathered together, (forasmuch as they be an assembly of men, whereof all be not governed with the Spirit and Word of God,) they may err, and sometimes have erred, even in things pertaining unto God. Wherefore things ordained by them as necessary to salvation have neither strength nor authority, unless it may be declared that they be taken out of holy Scripture.'

13.   'Perspicuitas.' Muller, *Dictionary of Latin and Greek Theological Terms*, 265.

understand **everything** [emphasis in the original] in the Bible.[14] A part of the reason today for this is evangelical misunderstanding.[15] What the clarity of Scripture does not mean, then, is that anyone and everyone can pick up the Word and understand everything in it as if it were a parenting book or an installation manual. The Scripture passage at the top of this chapter from Psalm 119 is a prayer for illumination. This means that it is a prayer asking for the grace of the Holy Spirit to open the heart to understand the Word. This presupposes that we don't understand.

Paul also spoke of illumination like this in Ephesians 1:

> That the God of our Lord Jesus Christ, the Father of glory, may give you the spirit of wisdom and of revelation in the knowledge of him, having the eyes of your hearts enlightened, that you may know what is the hope to which he has called you, what are the riches of his glorious inheritance in the saints, and what is the immeasurable greatness of his power toward us who believe (Eph. 1:17-19).

This was prayed by an apostle for believers! As one Greek Orthodox hymn evening hymn says:

1. Now at this evening hour,
O Thou, my Christ, to Thee,
Thou Word of God, Eternal Light,
All grateful praises be.

2. From Thee the Spirit comes,
Third beam of peerless light,
And in Thyself one glorious orb
The triple rays unite.

---

14. Joe Heschmeyer, "Six Reasons to Reject 'the Perspicuity of Scripture'" (April 13, 2013). As found at http://shamelesspopery.com/six-reasons-to-reject-the-perspicuity-of-scripture (Accessed August 22, 2022).

15. On this misunderstanding, see Gerry Breshears, "The Perspicuity of Scripture." As found at https://www.monergism.com/thethreshold/sdg/The%20 Perspicuity%20of%20Scripture%20by%20Gerry%20Breshears.pdf (Accessed August 22, 2022).

3. Thy word and wisdom Thou
To lighten man hast given,
That he the splendour might reflect
That shines superb in heaven.[16]

We see the need for understanding in the example of the Ethiopian eunuch (Acts 8). He read the words on his scroll containing Isaiah 53, but needed understanding of it. Why? Paul says elsewhere that 'our gospel is veiled…to those who are perishing' (2 Cor. 4:3). This means, first of all, that apart from the regenerating work of the Holy Spirit, no one can come to a saving knowledge of Christ. Then there is still the need for the illuminating work of the Spirit to understand the words on the page rightly. 'So, are you saying I shouldn't give a Bible to my unsaved neighbor?' No, that's *not* what I'm saying. We need to get the Scriptures into as many hands as possible, and pray that in reading them the Holy Spirit will do His work. The point is that apart from Him, no one – not even believers – can have a right understanding.

The clarity of Scripture also does not mean that there are no difficulties and obscure sayings in the Bible. In 1 Peter 1:10-12, Peter describes the Spirit-inspired prophets as reading their own scrolls to seek to understand whom they were speaking of. They saw the general shady outline of the coming Messiah, but they didn't see His face in the living color of His coming. Even prophets had limited understanding of the Word. Look also at 2 Peter 3:15-17. Again, Peter speaks this way, but this time of the apostle Paul himself: 'There are some things in them [Paul's letters] that are hard to understand' (v. 16). So one apostle had difficulty with another's writings. Do you want an example? If you've figured out who exactly the 'man of lawlessness' (2 Thess. 2:3) and 'he who now restrains' (2 Thess. 2:7) his coming are, then let me know!

The clarity of Scripture finally does not mean that all Scripture is equally clear. Not every verse is equally clear. Not every chapter is equally clear. Let me illustrate. Turn to Revelation 9 and read this mysterious chapter. Now go and read John 3:16. Which is clearer? This shows that not all passages are as clear as all other passages.

---

16.   *Hymns of the Greek Church,* trans. John Brownlie (Edinburgh and London: Oliphant, Anderson & Ferrier, 1900), 97.

## What the Clarity of Scripture Is

Restating our theme positively, *the Bible is clear (perspicuous) in matters relating to salvation and godliness.* To summarize Francis Turretin again, the clarity of Scripture means that what God's requires of sinners to be saved and how saved sinners are to live before God is so clearly taught in the Scriptures that these parts of the Word may be read and understood without the Pope.[17]

As I've been highlighting throughout these chapters, as a Reformed (catholic) Christian I want to follow my theological forebearers in seeking to conform my understanding of the Word with that of the early Church fathers. The ancients said things that the later Reformers picked up on and re-emphasized against the Roman Church; I want to speak the same way about Scripture. The Patriarch of Constantinople, John Chrysostom, said this:

> Therefore hath the grace of the Holy Spirit disposed and tempered them [the Scriptures] so, that publicans, and fishers, and tent-makers, shepherds, and the apostles, and simple men, and unlearned, might be saved by these books; that none of the simpler sort might make excuse by the hardness of them; and that such things as are spoken might be easy for all men to look on; that the labouring man, and the servant, the widow woman, and whosoever is most unlearned, may take some good, when they are read.[18]

According to Chrysostom, anyone can read the Bible and learn what it means to be saved. To use modern terms, it doesn't matter what your ethnic, socio-economic, or educational status is to know the Lord's will for your life in Scripture.

Tatian (120–180) was an Assyrian Christian and pupil of Justin Martyr. He is known for his 'Address to the Greeks' (*Oratio ad Graecos*), an early Christian apologetic for the Faith. In the *Oratio*, Tatian gave an account of his own conversion and provided his readers with an answer to the question of where a person can go who wishes to know what Christians believe. He told the story that he was converted by reading what he previously considered to be 'certain barbaric writings.' These Scriptures led him to conclude that the Christian faith was the true faith. He listed a number of criteria

---

17.  Turretin, *Institutes*, 1:143.
18.  Jewel, 'A Treatise of the Holy Scriptures,' *Works* 4:1183.

by which he judged Scripture to be superior to the writings of the pagans. As he said, when he read Scripture, his soul was 'taught of God' and he 'put faith' in what he read. He once was a practitioner of 'the mysteries' and 'religious rites' of the Romans (Jupiter) and Greeks (Artemis). Then he 'retir[ed] by myself, I sought how I might be able to discover the truth':

> I happened to meet with certain barbaric writings, too old to be compared with the opinions of the Greeks, and too divine to be compared with their errors; and I was led to put faith in these by the unpretending cast of the language, the inartificial character of the writers, the foreknowledge displayed of future events, the excellent quality of the precepts, and the declaration of the government of the universe as centred in one Being. And, my soul being taught of God, I discern that the former class of writings lead to condemnation, but that these put an end to the slavery that is in the world, and rescue us from a multiplicity of rulers and ten thousand tyrants, while they give us, not indeed what we had not before received, but what we had received but were prevented by error from retaining.[19]

One application of this principle of perspicuity is since what is necessary for salvation and godliness is clear in the Word, we, as believers, need to focus on these basic truths. There are some things necessary for us all to read and know and there are other things that are not. We make a distinction between *catholic articles* and *theological articles*, between those *things necessary for everyone to know for salvation* and those *things not necessary for everyone*, but reserved for ministers, professors, and elders to discuss.[20] I know you have probably never heard this, so let me spell it out. I will assume that you are the average church-going mom or dad. *You* don't need to worry yourself over which eschatological position you hold to. *You* don't need to have a position on the order of God's eternal decrees. *You* don't need to be an articulate spokesman for issues relating to the relationship between the Church and the broader culture, including the state. *You* don't need to know all the ins and outs of

---

19. Tatian, *Oratio ad Graecos* 29 in *Ante-Nicene Fathers*, trans. J.E. Ryland, ed. Alexander Roberts and James Donaldson, 10 vols. (1885; repr., Peabody, MA: Hendrickson Publishers, fourth printing 2004), 2:77 col. 1-2.

20. Maccovius, *Scholastic Discourse*, 71.

Christology (doctrine of Christ) and how it relates to medieval and Reformation debates surrounding the meaning of the Lord's Supper. To use an image from Gregory the Great (540–604), Scripture is a river that has both shallow and deep parts and in which lambs can walk and elephants can swim.[21] What perspicuity, therefore, means is that you need to keep your focus on reading the Word (see chapter 9) and delving into understanding with your mind and applying to your heart and will its basics. These have traditionally been summarized in

Christian catechesis (instruction) with the Apostles' Creed, the Ten Commandments, and the Lord's Prayer. Listen to Martin Luther:

> But this I say for myself. I am also a doctor and preacher, just as learned and experienced as all them who are so high and mighty. Nevertheless, each morning, and whenever else I have time, I do as a child who is being taught the catechism and I read and recite word for word the Lord's Prayer, the Ten Commandments, the Creed, and the Psalms, etc. I must still read and study the catechism daily, and yet I cannot master it as I wish, but must remain a child and pupil of the catechism – and I also do so gladly.[22]

## Conclusion: Using the Means to Understand Scripture's Basics

What does all this mean for us? If the Scriptures are clear in their teaching on what's necessary to be saved and how we are to live, we are to use the means that God has given us to understand these basic teachings throughout our lives. The Scriptures become clearer and dearer to us 'in a due use of the ordinary means' so that we 'may attain unto a sufficient understanding of them' (WCF 1.7).[23]

---

21.　Gregory the Great, *Morals on the Book of Job*, trans. Members of the English Church (Oxford: John Henry Parker, 1844), 1:9.

22.　Martin Luther, T*he Large Catechism*, in *The Annotated Luther: Volume 2, Word and Faith*, ed. Kirsi I. Sterna (Minneapolis: Fortress Press, 2015), 290-91.

23.　*Reformed Confessions: Volume 4*, 236.

What are these 'means'? Reading the Word daily. Praying for illumination: 'open my eyes that I may behold wondrous things out of your law' (Ps. 119:18). Meditating on the law of God 'day and night' (Ps. 1:2). Hearing it proclaimed week-in and week-out. When we do these things, we'll 'grow in the grace and knowledge of our Lord and Savior Jesus Christ' (2 Pet. 3:18) and be of use to Him as witnesses for His name in the world. A part of this growth is becoming confident in the Scriptures as God's Word and being able to express what they say to a lost and dying world.

# Chapter 9   READING THE WORD
## *He Shall Read It*

---

'And when he sits on the throne of his kingdom, he shall
write for himself in a book a copy of this law, approved
by the Levitical priests. And it shall be with him, and he
shall read in it all the days of his life, that he may learn to
fear the Lord his God by keeping all the words of this law
and these statutes, and doing them, that his heart may not
be lifted up above his brothers, and that he may not turn
aside from the commandment, either to the right hand or
to the left, so that he may continue long in his kingdom, he
and his children, in Israel' (Deut. 17:18-20).

In the Canadian newspaper, *The Globe and Mail*, one author described
'the collapse of the liberal church' in Canada and its equivalent
in America. The author spoke of a Synod (national assembly) of
the United Church of Canada, at which one of its main agenda
items was a resolution calling for the boycott of products from
Israeli settlements. She spoke of a Synod of The Episcopal Church
U.S.A., at which one of its main agenda items was allowing the
transgendered to become priests. Her conclusion was that 'people's
overall belief in God hasn't declined. What's declined is people's

participation in religion. With so little spiritual nourishment to offer, it's no wonder the liberal churches have collapsed.'[1]

If we want to remain relevant as Bible-receiving, Bible-believing, Bible-preaching, and Bible-reading churches, the key is to continue receiving, believing, preaching, and reading the Word of God! The Word *is* inherently relevant because it is God's Word. In it, we have 'the faith that was once for all delivered to the saints' (Jude 3). In it, we find that nourishment which our souls so desperately need in these dark days. So vital for our lives is the Word, that Chrysostom once said, 'If we must fight, they are a sword; if we hunger, they are meat; if we thirst, they are drink; if we have no dwelling-place, they are a house; if we be naked, they are a garment; if we be in darkness, they be light unto our going.'[2]

Deuteronomy 17 is a law about the king of Israel. One requirement for a godly king was that he utilized the law of God. He was to obtain a copy of the law from the priests and then copy out by hand his own copy. We read in 2 Kings 11 that Joash, the seven-year-old king of Judah, was coronated by the high priest Jehoida, who 'gave him the testimony' (v. 12). Then he was to read the law even after he entered the busyness of his office. He was not to be hindered. He was not to come up with excuses. He was also to meditate upon it, learning the fear of God throughout his life. Finally, he was to practice what he read. In the words of James, 'Be doers of the word, and not hearers only' (James 1:22).

What does this story of the king have to do with us? In 'the fulness of time' (Gal. 4:4) all the promises and prophecies, shadows and symbols of the Old Testament 'find their Yes in [Jesus]' (2 Cor. 1:20). One aspect of living under the New Covenant's 'betterness' (Heb. 6:9; 7:19, 22; 8:6; 9:23; 10:34; 11:16, 35, 40; 12:24) is that when we're united by faith to Jesus, our better prophet, priest, and king (Heidelberg Catechism, Q&A 31), we 'share in his anointing' by the Spirit to be prophets who 'confess his name,' priests who 'present [ourselves]…as a living sacrifice of thanks,' *and* kings who 'strive…against sin and the devil in this life, and afterward

---

1. Margaret Wente, 'The Collapse of the Liberal Church,' *The Globe and Mail* (July 28, 2012). As found at https://www.theglobeandmail.com/opinion/the-collapse-of-the-liberal-church/article4443228 (Accessed January 14, 2021).

2. Cited in Jewel, 'A Treatise of the Holy Scriptures,' *Works* 4:1177.

[will]…reign with Christ over all creation for eternity' (Heidelberg Catechism, Q&A 32). What once was a law only for the king is now applied to all of us as kings in Christ. Let's participate in our kingly calling by *reading the Word*.

## A High Privilege

Reading the Word is *a high privilege*. As far as I know, besides the Levitical priests, we read of no other individual apart from the king in all of the Old Testament being required to obtain a copy of the laws of God and to privately read them as Deuteronomy 17:18 describes. What a privilege the king had to obtain a copy of the law. What a privilege of actually copying the law out in his own handwriting. How his hand must have trembled in awe! How he must

have been amazed to read God's very word for himself! Gregory the Great once wrote a letter in which he said, 'Learn the heart of God in the words of God.'[3] Thomas Aquinas (1225–1274) said, 'Holy Scripture…manifests the heart of Christ.'[4] In reading the words of God we get a glimpse into God's very heart for us His people. The psalmist sang of this heart of the Lord: 'He declares his word to Jacob, his statutes and rules to Israel. He has not dealt thus with any other nation' (Ps. 147:19-20). Yet, it wasn't a daily practical privilege for ancient Israelites to read as it is for us.

Think for a moment about when you started learning to read. After you had listened to your parents reading to you for several years you started to learn the sounds yourself. Then you started to learn to sound out two and three letter words. Then you learned to read those words in a short sentence. After a while of doing that,

---

3.  *Letter to Theodorus*, 4:31 in *Nicene and Post-Nicene Fathers: Second Series*, trans; Charles Lett Feltoe, 14 vols. (1895; repr., Peabody, MA: Hendrickson Publishers, fourth printing 2004), 12:156 col. 2

4.  On Psalm 21:11, trans. Stephen Loughlin, The Aquinas Translation Project. As found at http://hosted.desales.edu/w4/philtheo/loughlin/ATP/Psalm_21.html (Accessed January 19, 2021).

you learned to understand what you were reading. Reading really is amazing! What's really amazing is that we get to do this with the Bible, God's own words to us. We all need to learn how to read our Bibles. Step by step like little children, we all need to come to the Lord in His Word and begin the process from learning letter sounds to understanding what we are reading.

## A Habitual Practice

Reading the Bible is to be a habitual practice. Deuteronomy 17:19 goes on to say, 'And it shall be with him, and he shall read in it all the days of his life.' The king, especially, was to be Israel's exemplar of the blessed man of Psalm 1, shunning the ways of sinners for the ways of the Lord that he meditated on in the law of God 'day and night' (Ps. 1:2). The Scriptures call upon us in the New Covenant to read the Word habitually. We are to do so publicly as congregations of believers, as families, and as individuals. Recently, the Canadian Archdiocese of the Orthodox Church described the state of biblical literacy among their people as 'abysmal ignorance.' In response, it wrote that Bible reading 'is vital; an absolute necessity of life.' This isn't a matter of polemical pride – we read, they don't – but of genuine thanks for the exhortation and as a caution to guards our hearts.[5]

*Publicly*

This was done in the ancient Jewish synagogue, as evidenced by Jesus entering the synagogue and reading the appointed passage from the prophet Isaiah (Luke 4:16-24). This was done in the apostolic Christian Church, as evidenced by Paul's words (1 Thess. 5:27; Col. 4:16) and John's words (Rev. 1:3). This continued in the ancient Church of the second century and beyond. For example, Justin Martyr said: 'And on the day called Sunday, all who live in cities or in the country gather together to one place, and the memoirs of the apostles or the writings of the prophets are read, as long as time permits.'[6] Tertullian (155–240) said: 'We assemble to read our

---

5. "Is Bible Reading Orthodox? Is Bible Study Orthodox?" As found at https://www.archdiocese.ca/content/bible-reading-orthodox-bible-study-orthodox (Accessed August 22, 2022).

6. *First Apology*, ch. 67.

sacred writings...with the sacred words we nourish our faith, we animate our hope, we make our confidence more steadfast.'[7]

*Familially*

If the Lord provides you with a family, read of the heart of God in the words of God with your family. Moses exhorted Israel, saying: 'these words that I command you today shall be on your heart. You shall teach them diligently to your children, and shall talk of them when you sit in your house, and when you walk by the way, and when you lie down, and when you rise' (Deut. 6:6-7). This practice of the covenant people was experienced by Timothy: 'But as for you, continue in what you have learned and have firmly believed, knowing from whom you learned it and how from childhood you have been acquainted with the sacred writings' (2 Tim. 3:14-15). Family Bible reading is necessary to propagate the Christian religion in our children. With all the studies and surveys constantly showing the rising generation in American churches leaving those churches,[8] is it any wonder when parents, especially fathers, are not taking the time to read the Word with their children? Jerome once said, 'Ignorance of the Scriptures is ignorance of Christ.'[9] Chrysostom said ignorance of Scripture is 'the cause of all evils' and like 'go[ing] into battle without arms [weapons].'[10]

*Privately*

We *get* to hear of God's love for us in His Word. So, let's love Him in return by reading His Word privately. Psalm 1 speaks of the singular, 'the man,' who is blessed because 'his delight is in the law of the LORD, and on his law he meditates day and night' (Ps. 1:1-2). Prophetically, this is Jesus, the second Adam (Rom. 5:12-21;

---

7. *Apology*, ch. 39.

8. For example, Ryan P. Burge, 'Only Half of Kids Raised Southern Baptist Stay Southern Baptist' *Christianity Today* (May 24, 2019). As found at https://www.christianitytoday.com/news/2019/may/southern-baptist-sbc-decline-conversion-retention-gss.html (Accessed January 14, 2021).

9. *ignoratio Scripturarum, ignoratio Christi est.* Jerome, 'Prologus,' *Commentariorum in Isaiam Prophetam, in Patrologia Linguae* 24, ed. J.–P. Migne (Paris: Apud Garnier Fratres, 1865), 17 col. 1.

10. Chrysostom, 'Homily 9 on Colossians,' in *Nicene and Post-Nicene Fathers: First Series,* ed. Philip Schaff, 14 vols. (1889; repr., Peabody, MA: Hendrickson Publishers, fourth printing 2004), 13:301 col. 1.

1 Cor. 15:21, 22, 45-49). As we saw above, in Him we receive all His blessings. According to Psalm 1, one of His blessings is to read the Word. To read the Word and meditate upon the Word as a believer causes one to be like a well-watered and fruitful tree (Ps. 1:3). Psalm 119 is also the meditation of an individual believer: 'Oh how *I* love your law! It is *my* meditation all the day' (Ps. 119:97). Meditating on the Word makes one wise (Ps. 119:98), makes one godly (Ps. 119:101), and gives us a spiritual delight as the Word is 'sweeter than honey to my mouth!' (Ps. 119:103) This is why 'to neglect [the reading of the Word] is to despise our own souls, and deprive ourselves of the advantage of God's instituted means of grace.'[11]

One benefit of daily habitual Bible reading is coming to a greater understanding of it when we then assemble with our church family to hear it preached. Chrysostom said:

> But in order that the word may be the more easy to learn, we pray and entreat you, as we have done also with respect to the other Scriptures, to take up beforehand that portion of the Scripture which we may be going to explain, that your reading may prepare the way for your understanding (as also was the case with the eunuch), and so may greatly facilitate our task.[12]

Another benefit is that over the course of our lives as children of God, we more and more become a walking and talking Bible. In the words of Paul, we are to be a 'living epistle' (2 Cor. 3:1-3).[13] Chrysostom praised his congregation in Constantinople for their zeal to hear him preach. Then he exhorted them to read the Word at home: 'continue to have the same zeal, and manifest it not here only, but that also when you are at home, you converse man with wife, and father with son.'[14]

---

11.　Watson, *Puritan Sermons*, 2:68.

12.　*The Homilies of S. John Chrysostom, Archbishop of Constantinople, on the Gospel of St. Matthew: Part I, Homilies I–XXV* (London: Walter Smith, 1885), 12.

13.　See also Watson, *Puritan Sermons*, 2:68.

14.　Chrysostom, 'Homily 3 on John,' in *Nicene and Post-Nicene Fathers: First Series*, ed. Philip Schaff, 14 vols. (1889; repr., Peabody, MA: Hendrickson Publishers, fourth printing 2004), 14:10 col. 1.

How are we to read the Word? The Westminster Larger Catechism gives us helpful guidance:

> The holy Scriptures are to be read with an high and reverent esteem of them; with a firm persuasion that they are the very Word of God, and that he only can enable us to understand them; with desire to know, believe, and obey the will of God revealed in them; with diligence, and attention to the matter and scope of them; with meditation, application, self-denial, and prayer. (Q&A 157)[15]

### With Reverence

Read *'with an high and reverent esteem of them.'* Let me put it to you like this: if we love reading our favorite author's books, how much more so should we have a love of the words of God Himself? If we love the letters, the sentences, the prose and poetry of human authors, how much more should we love those words that were inscribed with the finger of God and breathed out of His mouth?

In Deuteronomy 4:10, the Lord says: 'Gather the people *to me*, that I may let them hear *my words*, so that they may learn to fear *me*.' To hear the Word is to hear God Himself. While we distinguish between the Word of God written and the living Word of God spoken, the two have one thing in common: God. To hear the Word written is to hear the Word spoken by God. Therefore Thomas Watson (1620–1686) once said: 'Think every line you read God is speaking to you.'[16] As you read your Bible with reverence, consciously know that you are listening to the voice of God

*Thomas Watson.*

Himself. Because the Word is the Holy Spirit's love letter to us,[17] we should be humbled to the core and be in awe of the fact that of the billions of people in the world, *you – I –* have been given the Word!

---

15.  *Reformed Confessions: Volume 4*, 340–41.

16.  Watson, *Puritan Sermons*, 2:60.

17.  Ibid., 2:64.

*With Persuasiveness*

Read '*with a firm persuasion that they are the very Word of God, and that he only can enable us to understand them.*' We turn to the Scriptures because they are God's words to us. Persuaded of this, we should also be persuaded that He alone can make His words known to us. In the Psalms we read repeatedly lines like this: 'Open my eyes, that I may behold wondrous things out of your law.... Make me understand the way of your precepts.... Give me understanding that I may learn your commandments' (Ps. 119:18, 27, 73). We described this previously as the illumination of the Holy Spirit.

We believe in the Holy Spirit's inspiration of the Word but also in His illumination. Because inspiration is true, illumination is necessary, regardless of our intellect and ability to read a text. Thomas Ridgeley (1667–1734) said it like this: 'if God is not pleased to succeed our endeavours, we shall remain destitute of the experimental knowledge of divine truths, which is absolutely necessary to salvation.' This means that reading the Word is not only understanding with our heads the words on the page but knowing with our hearts, by the work of the Spirit, the meaning of those words *for me*. Like a child needs help understanding a book that he or she is reading and therefore goes to a parent or teacher for help, so too we need to go to God in prayer and ask Him to help us know what He is saying.

*With Earnestness*

Read '*with desire to know, believe, and obey the will of God revealed in them.*' When Moses called the Israelites to assemble to hear the words of the Lord, it was so that they would 'do them' (Deut. 4:1). This is vital for us to meditate upon. It's so easy for us to read the Word looking for doctrine, looking for the theological arguments the apostles make, and looking for the proofs we need to persuade others to believe in Christ. We so often focus on the word 'Word' when we speak of the '*Word* of God.' But don't forget that it is the Word *of God*. The Word is the means that God has chosen to reveal Himself to us. When you sit down to read it, then, you are coming not to an *it*, but to a *Him*. This should make us earnest and desirous to read because we are having fellowship with the Lord in the reading and in the doing.

*With Diligence*

Read *'with diligence, and attention to the matter and scope of them.'* You may not like learning English grammar – what's a subject, what's an object, what's a pronoun, or what's a noun. It can be tedious. Here in Southern California, a regular sight on the beach is a person with headphones on waving a metal detector back and forth over the sand. When a person first starts doing this, every little sound makes them think that they have found something valuable, so they bend down and dig it up. Over time, though, they learn to listen diligently to the distinct sounds of different kinds of metals. We need to learn how to read the Word with such diligence.

The ancient prophets 'searched and inquired carefully, inquiring what person or time the Spirit of Christ in them was indicating when he predicted the sufferings of Christ and the subsequent glories' (1 Peter 1:10-11). We need to read the Word with such diligence and careful inquiry. As Watson said, 'If one go over the scripture cursorily, there is little good to be got by it; but if he be serious in reading of it, it is the "savour of life".'[18]

*With Personalness*

Read *'with meditation, application, self-denial, and prayer.'* These are personal things. Moses spoke to a generation of Israelites who were not present at Mount Horeb, yet he said they were to teach their children and grandchildren 'how on the day that you stood before the LORD your God' (Deut. 4:10). How could they do that? The point was not that they were actually there, but that as they learned the words of God, they were personally to appropriate and to identify themselves with the Word.

The Word, then, is not some abstract thing 'out there.' As Paul says, it is to dwell deeply within us (Col. 3:16). We are to meditate on the Word – that is, to think intently and intensely about it. We are to do this more than we meditate on our fantasy football stats, the latest political polls, or our Christmas shopping list! If reading the Word gets God's truth into our heads, then meditating on it gets it into our hearts.

---

18. Watson, *Puritan Sermons*, 2:61.

### With Christ Always in View

If I may say this, there's one thing missing in the Larger Catechism's list of keys in reading the Word: Jesus Christ. He told the scribes that their searching in the Old Testament Scriptures for eternal life should have led them to Him: 'it is they that bear witness about me' (John 5:39). J.C. Ryle wrote movingly and simply of this truth: 'In every part of both Testaments Christ is to be found, – dimly and indistinctly at the beginning, – more clearly and plainly in the middle, – fully and completely at the end, – but really and substantially everywhere.'[19]

Christ's sacrifice and death for sinners, and Christ's kingdom and future glory, are the light we must bring to bear on any book of Scripture we read. Christ's cross and Christ's crown are the clue we must hold fast, if we would find our way through Scripture difficulties. Christ is the only key that will unlock many of the dark places of the Word. Some people complain that they do not understand the Bible. And the reason is very simple. They do not use the key. To them the Bible is like the hieroglyphics in Egypt. It is a mystery, just because they do not use the key.

> ...I charge every reader of this paper to ask himself frequently what the Bible is to him. Is it a Bible in which you have found nothing more than good moral precepts and sound advice? Or is it a Bible in which you have found Christ? Is it a Bible in which 'Christ is all'? If not, I tell you plainly, you have hitherto used your Bible to very little purpose. You are like a man who studies the solar system, and leaves out in his studies the sun, which is the centre of all. It is no wonder if you find your Bible a dull book![20]

By reading the Word in such a way, we will not only be informed in our hearts, but inflamed in our hearts. The more we learn about God's heart of love for us the more we should love Him in return. The more we love God the more we should become living epistles of His love for the world.

---

19.    J.C. Ryle, 'Christ Is All,' in *Holiness: Its Nature, Hindrances, Difficulties, and Roots* (London: William Hunt and Company, 1879), 441, 443-44.

20.    Ryle, 'Christ Is All,' in *Holiness*, 443–44.

## A Holy Purpose

Finally, in reading the Word we engage in *a holy purpose*. At the end of Deuteronomy 17:19 we learn the purpose of the king's reading the Word: 'that he may learn to fear the LORD his God by keeping all the words of this law and these statutes, and doing them, that his heart may not be lifted up' (vv. 19, 20). Our holy purpose in reading the Word is to delight in the Lord and to do the Lord's will.

### Delighting in the Lord

The purpose of my reading the Word is to delight in the Lord's love for me in His Word. Think about receiving a present. The word 'present' is another way of saying 'gift.' What's a gift? An act of grace. Someone gives you something not because you deserved it, but because they decided to express their love by it.

Ten times in the great Psalm of the Word of God, Psalm 119, we read of the psalmist praising the Lord for receiving the Lord's Word, saying he 'delights' in the Word (Ps. 119:14, 16, 24, 35, 47, 70, 77, 92, 143, 174). Why? Because the Word is the living Word *of the Lord* to us His people. The psalmist also describes his delight in the Word in comparison to other delightful things. He compares the Word to gold and silver: 'The law of your mouth is better to me than thousands of gold and silver pieces' (v. 72; cf. v. 127). He compares the Word to honey: 'How sweet are your words to my taste, sweeter than honey to my mouth!' (v. 103)

Elsewhere in Scripture, we read of the Word being compared to other things. The Word is compared to a sword that defends against spiritual enemies (Eph. 6:17). The Word is compared to a lamp that guideS us (Ps. 119:105). The Word is compared to milk that nourishes our souls (1 Pet. 2:2). If you love God, it's not just your *duty* to read the Word but your *delight to receive* it as the very Word of the true and living God.

### Doing the Lord's Will

The purpose of my reading the Word is also to do His will in response to His love for me in His Word. As we read the Word and meditate upon it, we experience the sanctifying power of the Word, which washes over us like water (Eph. 5:26). In Deuteronomy 4, the Lord exhorts His dear children to hear, to know, and to do

109

His Word. He exhorts them to 'listen to [his] statutes and [his] rules' (v. 1) and not to 'add to the word...that you may keep [his] commandments' (v. 2). He exhorts them to remember, 'I have taught you statutes and rules' so that they would 'do them' (vv. 5, 6). By doing them the nations would say, 'And what great nation is there, that has statutes and rules so righteous?' (v. 8) The practical benefit of this is 'that they may learn to fear me all the days that they live on the earth, and that they may teach their children so' (v. 10).

## Conclusion: Reading the Word as Spiritual Warfare

Let me conclude by saying that we are to read the Word as an act of spiritual warfare. It takes discipline and training. It takes honing our skills to use the Word. The greatest Reformation defense of the Word of God against the claims of the Roman Church was that of the Englishman, William Whitaker. He described the spiritual warfare we enter when we take up the Word in these words:

> Our arms shall be the sacred scriptures, that sword and shield of the word, that tower of David, upon which a thousand bucklers hang, and all the armour of the mighty, the sling and the pebbles of the brook wherewith David stretched upon the ground that gigantic and haughty Philistine.[21]

One practical way we experience this spiritual warfare is in discerning true from false doctrine. While we might think of false doctrine as just an idea, the New Testament says behind it are 'spirits' (e.g., Eph. 6:10-17; 2 Thes. 2:1-12; 1 John 4:1-6). In the late nineteenth century, J.C. Ryle asked, "What is the best safe-guard against false doctrine?—I answer in one word, 'The Bible: the Bible regularly read, regularly prayed over, regularly studied.'" In order to "wield [the sword of the Spirit] successfully, we must read it habitually, diligently, intelligently, and prayerfully."[22]

I want you to be confident that you hold the very Word of God in your hands. No Church, Pope, scholar, group of people, or the devil himself can change that fact. As Martin Luther said, 'A simple

---

21. Whitaker, *Disputation on Holy Scripture*, 19.

22. J.C. Ryle, *Knots Untied: Being Plain Statements on Disputed Points in Religion from the Standpoint of an Evangelical Churchman* (1877; repr., Cambridge: James Clarke & Co., 1977), 276.

layman armed with Scripture is to be believed above a pope or a council without it.'[23]

So pick up your Bible, as a sword, and learn to wield it in spiritual war by reading it, believing it, obeying it, and speaking it every day.

23.    Roland H. Bainton, *Here I Stand* (Nashville: Abingdon Press, 1950), 117.

## Chapter 10   EXPERIENCING THE WORD

## *Reviving the Soul*

---

The law of the LORD is perfect,
reviving the soul;
the testimony of the LORD is sure,
making wise the simple;
the precepts of the LORD are right,
rejoicing the heart;
the commandment of the LORD is pure,
enlightening the eyes;
the fear of the LORD is clean,
enduring forever;
the rules of the LORD are true,
and righteous altogether.
More to be desired are they than gold,
even much fine gold;
sweeter also than honey
and drippings of the honeycomb.
Moreover, by them is your servant warned;
in keeping them there is great reward (Ps. 19:7-11).

God has spoken in the Scriptures of the Old and New Testaments
(2 Tim. 3:16). This is the Christian confession. Another is perhaps
not as well known: the God who spoke, *speaks*. Do you have *this*

conviction, too? You and I don't have to be so over-reactive in rejecting extremes in the Charismatic and Pentecostal movements that it's as though God were silent to us. I know what that's like as a former Pentecostal youth pastor-turned Reformed pastor. I know 'cage phase' Calvinism well. But even us 'frozen chosen' types believe God still speaks to us audibly. He does so every time we read His Word, hear it read, and hear it preached (1 Thess. 2:13).

Did God speak in times of old? (Heb. 1:1-2) Absolutely. Does God still speak? We should be able to say the same 'absolutely!' But how is this the case? The answer is the Holy Spirit. The Westminster Larger Catechism says 'the *Spirit of God* maketh the reading, but especially the preaching of the Word, an effectual means' (Q&A 155).[1] One of the concerns of Roman Catholic and Orthodox friends you may have faced is that they see us focusing on the Bible merely as ink on paper. The *Catholic Catechism* says, 'the Christian faith is not a "religion of the book".' Instead, it is 'the religion of the "Word" of God.' Thus, 'If the Scriptures are not to remain a dead letter, Christ, the eternal Word of the living God, must, through the Holy Spirit, "open [our] minds to understand the Scriptures"' (Luke 24:45).[2] We affirm that it is the Holy Spirit who unites ancient texts with modern hearers. As the apostle Paul described it, 'the sword of the Spirit...is the word of God' (Eph. 6:17). It's not the bare Word read, the act of preaching itself, or especially the preacher, but the Holy Spirit who takes the Word written and causes it to be the Word living to our souls. Psalm 19 rejoices in this when it says that 'the law' is 'the law *of the* LORD,' 'the testimony' is 'the testimony *of the* LORD,' 'the precepts' are 'the precepts *of the* LORD,' 'the commandment' is 'the commandment *of the* LORD,' and 'the rules' are 'the rules *of the* LORD.' Yes, like Augustine once prayed, 'Your Scriptures are my pure delights,'[3] we love our Bibles. We do so because this is where we hear our God speak to us with certainty in an age of noise. Indeed, it was Pope Paul VI who said so beautifully, 'in the sacred books, the Father who is in heaven meets His children with great love and speaks with them.'[4]

---

1.   *Reformed Confessions: Volume 4*, 340.

2.   *Catechism of the Catholic Church*, 108, p. 37.

3.   Augustine, *Confessions* 11.2.3 in *Confessions: Books 9–13*, 193.

4.   *Dei Verbum*, 6.21. As found at http://www.vatican.va/archive/hist_councils/ii_vatican_council/documents/vat-ii_const_19651118_dei-verbum_en.html (Accessed January 22, 2021). See also *Catechism of the Catholic Church* 104, p. 36.

It's Scripture as the medium of God's presence that we cherish most of all. The Bible is not a dead letter. Personally, we can relate to stories like that of Augustine who experienced the Lord through the Word. In his autobiographical *Confessions* he told a story that he had fallen into darkness and went astray from the Lord. Yet, it was while at a distance from the Lord that he constantly heard the voice of the Lord behind calling him to return. When he returned, he prayed:

> ...I am returning, hot and thirsty to drink at your fountain... let me drink from it, and hereafter let me live. Let me not be my own life; from my own self I have lived badly. To myself I was death: but in you I begin to come to life again. Converse with me, commune with me; I have believed in your holy books, and their words are full of mystery.[5]

Not only do we personally experience the living presence of the Lord through His Word written, we also do so when we hear His living Word proclaimed from the written Word. Chrysostom related in a sermon the misunderstanding of what people hear when they come together as a church: 'They think that when they enter in here [the church], that they enter into our presence [the clergy], they think that they hear from us.' Preaching is not a *pastor's* thoughts, however pious. 'They do not lay to heart, they do not consider that they are entering the presence of God, that it is *He* who addresses them.... If they knew that it was God who through His prophet speaks these things, they would cast away all their pride.' He then made the analogy between rulers and God: 'For if rulers are addressing them, they do not allow their minds to wander, much else would they when God is speaking.' In conclusion, he movingly said:

> 'They think that when they enter in here [the church], that they enter into our presence [the clergy], they think that they hear from us.'[6]

> 'They do not lay to heart, they do not consider that they are entering the presence of God, that it is He who addresses them.... If they knew that it was God who through His

---

5. Augustine, *Confessions* 12.10.10 in *Confessions: Books 9–13*, 275.

6. Chrysostom, 'Homily 3 on 2 Thessalonians,' in Nicene and Post-Nicene Fathers: First Series, ed. Philip Schaff, 14 vols. (1889; repr., Peabody, MA: Hendrickson Publishers, fourth printing 2004), 13:387 col. 2.

prophet speaks these things, they would cast away all their pride.'[7]

'For if rulers are addressing them, they do not allow their minds to wander, much else would they when God is speaking.'[8]

We are ministers, beloved. We speak not our own things, but the things of God. Letters coming from heaven are read every day.... These letters are sent from God; therefore let us enter with becoming reverence into the churches and let us hearken with fear to the things here said.[9]

Let's consider how the presence and power of the Spirit works causing us to *experience the Word*.

## To Effect My Recognition of Sin

The presence and power of the Spirit work through the Word to effect my recognition of sin in my life. By the Word He enlightens my understanding of sin, convicts me of it, and humbles me under it.

In Psalm 19 we have the prayer of believing David. In his meditation on the effectiveness of the Word he says, 'The commandment of the LORD is pure, *enlightening* the eyes.' The Word of God enlightens, that is, opens our eyes to the reality of who we are, what's within us, and what we've done (Ps. 19:12-13). 'But I already know I'm a sinner and have already trusted in Jesus.' Sadly, this is a common objection of professing and practicing evangelicals. In response, think of a farmer. Does a farmer only remove the rocks from his field, break up his ground, prepare his soil, and weed only once before planting seeds that lead to a harvest? No. He must constantly do all these things. In the same way we need the Holy Spirit constantly to open our eyes to our sins as we read and hear the Word (see 1 John 1:5–2:2).

This is also obviously true for unbelievers. It's an assumption in the New Testament – I pray it becomes more so especially in our churches – that unbelievers will be in the midst of God's people in public worship. In 1 Corinthians 14 Paul contrasts what happens

---

7. Chrysostom, *'Homily 3 on 2 Thessalonians,'* NPNF: First Series), 13:387 col. 2.

8. Chrysostom, *'Homily 3 on 2 Thessalonians,'* NPNF: First Series), 13:387 col. 2.

9. Chrysostom, *'Homily 3 on 2 Thessalonians,'* NPNF: First Series), 13:387 col. 2–388 col, 1.

when unbelievers enter a church in which there are 'tongues.' Now, stay with me even though I take these to be the miraculous gifting of the Holy Spirit for someone to speak a language that was foreign to them. Paul contrasts this with a church in which there is prophecy, which I take as preaching in a known language[10]:

> If, therefore, the whole church comes together and all speak in tongues, and outsiders or unbelievers enter, will they not say that you are out of your minds? But if all prophesy, and an unbeliever or outsider enters, he is convicted by all, he is called to account by all, the secrets of his heart are disclosed, and so, falling on his face, he will worship God and declare that God is really among you (1 Cor. 14:23-25).

Paul deals with Christian worship ('the whole church comes together') and what happens when 'outsiders or unbelievers enter' (v. 23). He contrasts what we might call today two 'visitor experiences.' In the first, 'all [in the congregation] speak in tongues' and the response of the visiting unbeliever is to say 'you are out of your minds' (v. 23). Why? Because as I understand it, the unbeliever can't understand a word anyone is saying since they're all speaking in Spirit-given

---

10. This is not the place for me to get into these issues, so if you would like to explore this more, I recommend:

- For a strict 'cessationist' view (in chronological order): William Goode, *The Modern Claims to the Possession of the Extraordinary Gifts of the Spirit, Stated and Examined* (London: J. Hatchard and Son, 1833).
- Benjamin B. Warfield, *Counterfeit Miracles* (1918; repr, Edinburgh: The Banner of Truth Trust, 1976); Richard B. Gaffin, Jr., *Perspectives on Pentecost: New Testament Teaching on the Gifts of the Holy Spirit* (Phillipsburg, NJ: The Presbyterian and Reformed Publishing Company, 1979); O. Palmer Robertson, *The Final Word: A Biblical Response to the Case for Tongues and Prophecy Today* (Edinburgh: The Banner of Truth Trust, 1993).
- For a more cautious 'cessationist' view: Anthony A. Hoekema, *What About Tongue-Speaking?* (Grand Rapids: William B. Eerdmans Publishing Company, 1966).
- For a Calvinistic 'continuationist' view: Martyn Lloyd-Jones, *Joy Unspeakable: Power & Renewal in the Holy Spirit*, ed. Christopher Catherwood (Wheaton: Harold Shaw Publishers, 1984).
- For what I'd call an 'ordinarily these gifts have ceased, God can do what He wants, and we can't explain everything' view, see J. I. Packer, *Keep in Step with the Spirit* (1984; Grand Rapids: Fleming H. Revell, twelfth printing 2002).
- For exegesis of 1 Corinthians 12–14: D. A. Carson, *Showing the Spirit: A Theological Exposition of 1 Corinthians 12–14* (1987; Grand Rapids: Baker Books, sixth printing 2000); Rowland S. Ward, *Blessed by the Presence of the Spirit: The Authentic Charismatic Church* (Wantirna, Australia: New Melbourne Press, 1997).

foreign languages. In the second, 'all [in the congregation] prophesy' and the response of the visiting unbeliever is to be 'convicted by all [in the congregation prophesying]' (v. 24). Why? Because, again, as I understand it, prophesying is Spirit-empowered forth-telling (proclamation) of the Word with such power that the visiting unbeliever is 'called to account by all' and 'the secrets of his heart are disclosed' (vv. 24, 25). The result is that 'falling on his face, he will worship God and declare that God is really among you' (v. 25). What is the means the Holy Spirit uses to convict and convert sinners? His living and active Word.

## To Effect My Reception of the Savior

The presence and power of the Spirit work through the Word to effect my recognition of the Savior. Just like He caused the unbelieving visitor in Corinth, so He uses the Word to drive me out of myself and to draw me to Jesus Christ.

Psalm 19 says that 'the law of the LORD is perfect, reviving the soul; the testimony of the LORD is sure, making wise the simple' (v. 7). The Word of God has a reviving effect because it causes life to come from death, not only once and for all to those dead in their sins (Eph. 2:1) but to the believer in times of deep struggle with sin (Rom. 7). Augustine, again, said: 'in you I begin to come to life again. Converse with me, commune with me; I have believed in your holy books, and their words are full of mystery.'[11] The Word of God has a wising up effect because it causes those who are wise in themselves to be wise in Christ. Paul reminded Timothy to 'continue in what you have learned and have firmly believed' (2 Tim. 3:14). What was that? His being 'acquainted with the sacred writings, which are able to make you wise for salvation through faith in Christ Jesus' (2 Tim. 3:15).

In the Word, the Holy Spirit doesn't only shout out, 'Fire!' He also stands up in the midst of the danger and directs people to the safe exit. Think about Peter's Pentecost sermon. Afterwards we read, 'Now when they heard this, they were pricked in their heart, and said unto Peter and to the rest of the apostles, Men and brethren, what shall we do?' (Acts 2:37 KJV). Peter didn't leave them under guilt, but he pointed them to the grace of Jesus Christ. The Holy Spirit speaks to you in the Word of the danger of eternal hell-fire,

---

11.  Augustine, *Confessions* 12.10.10 in *Confessions: Books 9–13*, 275.

but He also speaks to you of the way of escape in Jesus because He experienced that hell-fire for you on the cross! '...during his whole life on earth, but especially at the end, Christ sustained in body and soul the wrath of God against the sin of the whole human race...in order that, he might deliver us, body and soul, from eternal condemnation' (Heidelberg Catechism, Q&A 37).[12]

## To Effect My Realization of Sanctification

The presence and power of the Spirit work through the Word to effect my realization of sanctification. When we read His Word and hear it preached to us with faith, the Holy Spirit works to sanctify us by His power and grace.

First, the Spirit uses the Word to conform me to the image of Jesus (Rom. 8:29). Think of yourself as a piece of hardwood encased in thick bark. Little by little the Spirit chips away, whittles you down, and sands you into a beautiful piece of art. But don't think of this conforming work as merely your outward life. No, this is His subduing your will to come into alignment with Jesus. He prayed, 'not my will, but yours, be done' (Luke 22:42), and so united to Him, we pray, 'Thy will be done on earth, as it is in heaven.'

Second, the Spirit uses the Word to strengthen me against all the corruptions, seduction, and temptations so prevalent not just in the world but also in my own sinful nature (Eph. 3:16). Because of what Jesus has done for us both to justify and to sanctify us (Rom. 5–6), we willingly submit to Him. Because of what we believe about God, we understand what we are to be because we have been liberated from being 'slaves of sin' to being 'slaves of obedience' (Rom. 6:16), to being 'slaves of righteousness' (Rom. 6:18), and to being 'slaves of God' (Rom. 6:22). In the words of the *Book of Common Prayer*, we are now obedient to the God 'whose service is perfect freedom.' What are we to be as slaves? What is our service? It's a loving obedience to God as outlined by the Ten Commandments. We are to love God above all else and love our neighbor with an equal love as we love ourselves. It is also diligent use of God's outward and ordinary means of grace. We are to have a jealous devotion to the Word of God. We are to have a thankful reception of the

---

12.   On this Q&A, see Daniel R. Hyde, *In Defense of the Descent: A Response to Contemporary Critics*, Explorations in Reformed Confessional Theology (Grand Rapids: Reformation Heritage Books, 2010).

sacraments. We are to be committed to offering up our desires to God in prayer.

Third, the Spirit uses the Word to build us up in grace by restoring, confirming, strengthening, and establishing our hearts in holiness and comfort through faith (1 Pet. 5:10). This work He does throughout this life until the life of the world to come.

These all-encompassing aspects and angles of our sanctification are expressed in Paul's aforementioned magisterial definition of the Word's inspiration. Not only is 'all Scripture....breathed out by God,' but it is also 'profitable for teaching, for reproof, for correction, and for training in righteousness.' The goal of this breathed-out Word is 'that the man of God may be complete, equipped for every good work' (2 Tim. 3:16-17). In other words, reading and studying the Word is not merely an intellectual exercise. Our minds, wills, and affections need to be engaged:

> We may know the Bible intellectually, and have no doubt about the truth of its contents. We may have our memories well stored with its leading texts, and be able to talk glibly about its leading doctrines. And all the time the Bible may have no influence over our hearts, and wills, and consciences. We may, in reality, be nothing better than the devils.[13]

Fourth, the Spirit uses the Word in my spiritual struggle against Satan. I know, we modern people are too enlightened and sophisticated to believe in actual demons that actually impact our lives. But this is what Paul teaches in Ephesians 6:10-18. The devil has many 'schemes' (v. 11), but we are to stand against them. We 'wrestle' him (v. 12), but not in an earthly way but heavenly, spiritual way. The devil shoots 'flaming darts' at us (v. 16); but we fight back with a sword. Paul calls it 'the sword of the Spirit' (v. 17), meaning, the sword that comes *from* the Spirit. How so? He goes on the describe what exactly this sword is: 'which is the word of God' (v. 17). The sword of the Word comes *from* the Spirit because he 'inspired' their words as we've already seen (2 Tim. 3:16-17). The word of God is His word! This is why we can stand so confidently against Satan in our daily spiritual struggle. Athanasius once recounted a story he heard from an older wise man that 'in old days in Israel they put daemons to flight by reading of the Scriptures only.' Athanasius then

---

13.   J.C. Ryle, *Expository Thoughts on the Gospels: Luke, Volume 2*, 125.

said, "daemons fear the words of holy men and cannot bear them; for the Lord Himself is in the words of Scripture and Him they cannot bear." Let us engage the spiritual war that surrounds us on all sides by taking up the sword the Holy Spirit has given us to fight with![14]

## Conclusion

You and I can find God's Word in our time. We can be certain that He has spoken and that He continues to speak. God is a God of revelation, making Himself known. Through the ages He has revealed Himself by speaking, but especially He has inspired patriarchs, prophets, and apostles to write His Word for generations to come. This inspired Word written is His authoritative Word to humanity until Jesus comes again. These inspired and authoritative words are contained in the canon of the Old and New Testament Scriptures. They're sufficient and perspicuous (clear) for salvation and living to God's glory.

This is why Christians need to read the Word daily and hear the Word read publicly weekly. When we do so, the Spirit speaks to us the living and active Word of God (Heb. 4:12). His Word comes to us in convicting Law, comforting Gospel, and conforming sanctification, all by the power of the Spirit. In the words of Thomas Watson, "The word is both a glass to show us the spots of our soul, and a laver to wash them away. The word has a transforming virtue in it; it irradiates the mind, and consecrates the heart."[15]

I pray this little book enables your heart and mind to grow in confidence in the Sacred Scriptures of the Old and New Testaments; and being confident in them, to apply them in you so that you may be a useful tool in the Lord's work in His vineyard of the world.

---

14. Athanasius, Letter to Marcellinus on the Interpretation of the Psalms. As found at https://www.theologyethics.com/2016/08/22/the-letter-of-athanasius-to-marcellinus-on-the-interpretation-of-the-psalms (Accessed August 22, 2022). For more on the theme of Scripture in our spiritual struggle with demonic forces, see Evagrius of Pontus, *Talking Back: A Monastic Handbook for Combating Demons*, trans. David Brakke (Collegeville, MNL Liturgucal Press, 2009).

15. Thomas Watson, *A Body of Practical Divinity* (Aberdeen: D. Chalmer and Co., 1838), 225 col. 1.

# Appendix 1

## *John Chrysostom on Daily Bible Reading*[1]

I am ever urging, and shall not cease to urge, that you give attention, not only to the words spoken [in preaching], but that also, when at home in your house, you exercise yourselves constantly in reading the Divine Scriptures. This, also, I have never ceased to press upon those who come to me privately. Let not any one say to me that these exhortations are vain and irrelevant, for 'I am constantly busy in the courts,' (suppose him to say;) 'I am discharging public duties; I am engaged in some art or handiwork; I have a wife; I am bringing up my children; I have to manage a household; I am full of worldly business; it is not for me to read the Scriptures, but for those who have bid adieu to the world, for those who dwell on the summit of the hills; those who constantly lead a secluded life [meaning, monks].'

What dost thou say, O man? Is it not for thee to attend to the Scriptures, because thou art involved in numerous cares? It is thy duty even more than theirs, for they do not so much need the aid to be derived from the Holy Scriptures as they do who are engaged

---

1.   *Four Discourses of Chrysostom. Chiefly on the Parable of the Rich Man and Lazarus,* trans. F. Allen (London: Longmans, Green, Reader, and Dyer, 1869), 60-68. Formatted for ease of reading.

in much business. For those who lead a solitary life, who are free from business and from the anxiety arising from business, who have pitched their tent in the wilderness, and have no communion with any one, but who meditate at leisure on wisdom, in that peace that springs from repose – *they*, like those who lie in the harbor, enjoy abundant security. But ourselves, who, as it were, are tossed in the midst of the sea, cannot avoid many failings, we ever stand in need of the immediate and constant comfort of the Scriptures. *They* rest far from the strife, and, therefore, escape many wounds; but *you* stand perpetually in the array of battle, and constantly are liable to be wounded: on this account, you have more need of the healing remedies. For, suppose, a wife provokes, a son causes grief, a slave excites to anger, an enemy plots against us, a friend is envious, a neighbor is insolent, a fellow-soldier causes us to stumble – or often, perhaps, a judge threatens us, poverty pains us, or loss of property causes us trouble, or prosperity puffs us up, or misfortune overthrows us; – there are surrounding us on all sides many causes and occasions of anger, many of anxiety, many of dejection or grief, many of vanity or pride; from all quarters, weapons are pointed at us. Therefore it is that there is need continually of the whole armor of the Scriptures. For, 'understand,' it says, 'that thou passest through the midst of snares, and walkest on the battlements of a city' (Ecclus. 9:13). The lusts of the flesh also more grievously afflict those who are engaged in the midst of business. For a noble appearance and beautiful person gain power over us through the eyes; and wicked words, entering by the ears, trouble our thoughts. Often, also, a well-modulated song softens the constancy of the mind. But why do I say these things? For that which seems to be weaker than all these, even the odor of sweet scents from the meretricious throng with whom we meet, falling upon the senses, entrances us, and, by this chance accident, we are made captive.

Many other such things there are that beset our soul; and we have need of the divine remedies that we may heal wounds inflicted, and ward off those which, though not inflicted, would else be received in time to come – thus quenching afar off the darts of Satan, and shielding ourselves by the constant reading of the Divine Scriptures.

It is not possible – I say, it is not possible, for any one to be secure without constant supplies of this spiritual instruction. Indeed, we may congratulate ourselves, if, constantly using this remedy, we ever are able to attain salvation. But when, though each day receiving wounds, we make use of no remedies, what hope can there be of salvation?

Do you not notice that workmen in brass, or goldsmiths, or silversmiths, or those who engage in any art whatsoever, preserve carefully all the instruments of their art; and if hunger come, or poverty afflict them, they prefer to endure anything rather than sell for their maintenance any of the tools which they use. It is frequently the case that many thus choose rather to borrow money to maintain their house and family, than part with the least of the instruments of their art. This they do for the best reasons; for they know that when those are sold, all their skill is rendered of no avail, and the entire groundwork of their gain is gone. If those are left, they may be able, by persevering in the exercise of their skill, in time to pay off their debts; but if they, in the meantime, allow the tools to go to others, there is, for the future, no means by which they can contrive any alleviation of their poverty and hunger. We also ought to judge in the same way. As the instruments of their art are the hammer and anvil and pincers, so the instruments of our work are the apostolic and prophetic books, and all the inspired and profitable Scriptures. And as they, by their instruments, shape all the articles they take in hand, so also do we, by our instruments, arm our mind, and strengthen it when relaxed, and renew it when out of condition. Again, artists display their skill in beautiful forms, being unable to change the material of their productions, or to transmute silver into gold, but only to make their figures symmetrical. But it is not so with thee, for thou hast a power beyond theirs – receiving a vessel of wood, thou canst make it gold. And to this St. Paul testifies, speaking thus: 'In a great house there are not only vessels of gold and of silver, but also of wood and of earth. If a man therefore purge himself from these, he shall be a vessel unto honor, sanctified and meet for the master's use, and prepared unto every good work' (2 Tim. 2:20-21). Let us then not neglect the possession of the sacred books, that we receive no fatal injuries. Let us not hoard gold, but lay up, as our treasures, these inspired books. For gold, whenever it becomes abundant, causes trouble to its possessors; but these books, when carefully preserved, afford great benefit to those who possess them. As also where royal arms are stored, though no one should use them, they afford great security to those who dwell there; since neither thieves nor burglars, nor any other evil-doers, dare attack that place. In the same way, where the inspired books are, from thence all satanical influence is banished, and the great consolation of right principles comes to those who live there; yea, even the very sight of these books by itself makes us slower to commit iniquity. Even if we attempt any forbidden thing, and make ourselves unclean, when we return home and see these books, our conscience accuses us more keenly, and we become less likely to fall again into the same sins. Again, if we have been steadfast in our integrity, we gain more benefit, (if we are acquainted with the word;) for as soon as one comes to the gospel, he by a mere look both rectifies his understanding and ceases from all worldly cares. And if careful reading also follows, the soul, as if initiated in sacred mysteries, is thus purified and made better, while holding converse with God through the Scriptures.

'But what,' say they, 'if we do not understand the things we read?' Even if you do not understand the contents, your sanctification in a high degree results from it. However, it is impossible that all these things should alike be misunderstood; for it was for this reason that the grace of the Holy Spirit ordained that tax-gatherers, and fishermen, and tent-makers, and shepherds, and goatherds, and uninstructed and illiterate men, should compose these books, that no untaught man should be able to make this pretext; in order that the things delivered should be easily comprehended by all – in order that the handicraftsman, the domestic, the widow, yea, the most unlearned of all men, should profit and be benefited by the reading. For it is not for vain-glory, as men of the world, but for the salvation of the hearers, that they composed these writings, who, from the beginning, were endued with the gift of the Holy Ghost.

For those without – philosophers, rhetoricians, and annalists, not striving for the common good, but having in view their own renown – if they said anything useful, even this they involved in their usual obscurity, as in a cloud. But the apostles and prophets always did the very opposite; they, as the common instructors of the world, made all that they delivered plain to all men, in order that every one, even unaided, might be able to learn by the mere reading. Thus also the prophet spoke before, when he said, 'All shall be taught of God' (Isa. 54:13). 'And they shall no more say, every one to his neighbor, "Know the Lord," for they shall all know me, from the least to the greatest' (Jer. 31:34). St. Paul also says, 'And I, brethren, when I came to you, came not with excellency of speech, or of wisdom, declaring unto you the mystery of God' (1 Cor. 2:1). And again, 'My speech and my preaching was not with enticing words of man's wisdom, but in demonstration of the Spirit and of power' (1 Cor. 2:4). And again, 'We speak wisdom,' it is said, 'but not the wisdom of this world, nor of the princes of this world that come to naught' (1 Cor. 2:6). For to whom is not the gospel plain? Who is it that hears, 'Blessed are the meek; blessed are the merciful; blessed are the pure in heart,' and such things as these, and needs a teacher in order to understand any of the things spoken?

'But,' (it is asked), 'are the parts containing the signs and wonders and histories also clear and plain to every one?' This is a pretence, and an excuse, and a mere cloak of idleness. You do not understand the contents of the book? But how can you ever understand, while you are not even willing to look carefully? Take the book in your hand. Read the whole history; and, retaining in your mind the easy parts, peruse frequently the doubtful and obscure parts; and if you are unable, by frequent reading, to understand what is said, go to some one wiser; betake yourself to a teacher; confer with him about the things said. Show great eagerness to learn: then, when God sees that you are using such diligence, He will not disregard your perseverance and carefulness; but if no human being can teach you that which you seek to know, He Himself will reveal the whole.

Remember the eunuch of the queen of Ethiopia. Being a man of a barbarous nation, occupied with numerous cares, and surrounded on all sides by manifold business, he was unable to understand that which he read. Still, however, as he was seated in the chariot, he was reading. If he showed such diligence on a journey, think how diligent he must have been at home: if while on the road he did not let an opportunity pass without reading, much more must this have been the case when seated in his house; if when he did not fully understand the things he read, he did not cease from reading, much more would he not cease when able to understand. To show that he did not understand the things which he read, hear that which Philip said to him: 'Understandest thou what thou readest?' (Acts 8:30). Hearing this question he did not show provocation or shame: but confessed his ignorance, and said: 'How can I, except some man should guide me?' (Acts 8:31). Since therefore, while he had no man to guide him, he was thus reading; for this reason, he quickly received an instructor. God knew his willingness, He acknowledged his zeal, and forthwith sent him a teacher.

But, you say, Philip is not present with us now. Still, the Spirit that moved Philip is present with us. Let us not, beloved, neglect our own salvation! 'All these things are written for our admonition upon whom the ends of the world are come' (Rom. 10:11). The reading of the Scriptures is a great safeguard against sin; ignorance of the Scriptures is a great precipice and a deep gulf; to know nothing of the Scriptures, is a great betrayal of our salvation. This ignorance is the cause of heresies;[2] *this* it is that leads to dissolute living; *this* it is that makes all things confused. It is impossible, – I say, it is impossible, that any one should remain unbenefited who engages in persevering and intelligent reading. For see how much one parable has profited us! how much spiritual good it has done us! For many I know well have departed, bearing away abiding profit from the hearing; and if there be some who have not reaped so much benefit, still for that day on which they heard these things, they were rendered in every way better. And it is not a small thing

---

2. See also his Intro Homily on Romans: 'From this it is that countless evils have arisen – from ignorance of the Scriptures; from this it is that the plague of heresies has broken out; from this it is that there are negligent lives; from this there are labors without advantage. For as men deprived of this daylight would not walk aright, so they that look not to the gleaming of the Holy Scriptures must be frequently and constantly sinning, in that they are walking in the worst darkness.'

to spend one day in sorrow on account of sin, and in consideration of the higher wisdom, and in affording the soul a little breathing time from worldly cares. If we can effect this at each assembly without intermission, the continued hearing would work for us a great and lasting benefit.

# Appendix 2

# J.C. Ryle's 'Short Hints' on Bible Reading[1]

This tract may fall into the hands of someone who is willing to begin reading the Bible, but wants advice on the subject. Reader, are you that man? Listen to me, and I will give you a few short hints.

## 1. Begin Reading Your Bible this Very Day

The way to do a thing is to do it, and the way to read the Bible is actually to read it. It is not meaning, or wishing, or resolving, or intending, or thinking about it, which will advance you one step. You must positively read. There is no royal road in this matter, any more than in the matter of prayer. If you cannot read yourself, you must persuade somebody else to read it to you. But one way or another, through eyes or ears, the words of Scripture must actually pass before your mind.

## 2. Read the Bible with an Earnest Desire to Understand It

Think not for a moment, that the great object is to turn over a certain quantity of printed paper, and that it matters nothing whether you understand it or not. Some ignorant people seem to fancy that all is done, if they clear off so many chapters every day, though they may not have a notion what they are all about, and only know that they

---

1.    J.C. Ryle, *How Readest Thou? A Question for 1853* (London: Wertheim & Macintosh, 1853), 40-43. Formatted for ease of reading.

have pushed on their mark so many leaves. This is turning Bible reading into a mere form. It is almost as bad as the Popish habit of buying indulgences, by saying a fabulous number of *Ave Marias* and *Paternosters*. It reminds one of the poor Hottentot, who ate up a Dutch hymn-book, because he saw it comforted his neighbors' hearts. Settle it down in your mind, as a general principle, that a Bible not understood is a Bible that does no good. Say to yourself often as you read, *'What is this all about?'* Dig for the meaning like a man digging for Australian gold. Work hard, and do not give up the work in a hurry.

## 3. Read the Bible with Deep Reverence

Say to your soul, whenever you open the Bible, 'O my soul, thou art going to read a message from God.' The sentences of judges, and the speeches of kings, are received with awe and respect. How much more reverence is due to the words of the Judge of judges, and King of kings! Avoid, as you would cursing and swearing, that irreverent habit of mind, which some German divines have unhappily taken up the Bible. They handle the contents of the holy book as carelessly and disrespectfully, as if the writers were such as themselves. They make one think of a child composing a book to expose the fancied ignorance of his own father, – or of a pardoned murderer criticizing the hand-writing and style of his own reprieve. Enter rather into the spirit of Moses on Mount Horeb: 'Put they shoes from off thy feet; the place whereon thou standest is holy ground.'

## 4. Read the Bible with Earnest Prayer for the Teaching and Help of the Holy Spirit

Here is the rock on which many make shipwreck at the very outset. They do not ask for wisdom and instruction, and so they find the Bible dark, and carry nothing away from it. You should pray for the Spirit to guide you into all truth. You should beg the Lord Jesus Christ to open your understanding, as He did that of His disciples. The Lord God, by whose inspiration the book was written, keeps the keys of the book, and alone can enable you to understand it profitably. Nine times over in one Psalm, does he say, 'Give me understanding.' Well says Owen, there is a sacred light in the word: but there is a covering and veil on the eyes of men, so that they cannot behold it aright. Now the removal of this veil is the peculiar work of the Holy Spirit.' Humble prayer will throw more light on your Bible, than Poole's Synopsis, or all the commentaries that ever were written. Remember this, and say always, 'O God, for Christ's sake, give me the teaching of the Holy Spirit.'

## 5. Read the Bible with Child-Like Faith and Humility

Open your heart as you open God's book, and say, *'Speak, Lord, for thy servant heareth!'* Resolve to believe implicitly whatever you find there, however much it may run counter to your own prejudices. Resolve to receive heartily every statement of truth, whether you like it or not. Beware of that miserable habit into which some readers of the Bible fall. They receive some doctrines, because they like them. They reject others, because they are condemning to themselves, or to some lover, or relation, or friend. At this rate the Bible is useless. Are we to be judges of what ought to be in the Word? Do we know better than God? Settle it down in your mind that you will receive all, and believe all, and that what you cannot understand you will take on trust. Remember, when you pray, you are speaking to God, and God hears you. But, remember, when you read, God is speaking to you, and you are not to answer again, but to listen.

## 6. Read the Bible in a Spirit of Obedience and Self-Application

Sit down to the study of it with a daily determination that you will live by its rules, rest on its statements, and act on its commands. Consider, as you travel through every chapter, *'How does this affect my thinking and daily conduct? What does this teach me?'* It is poor work to read the Bible from mere curiosity and speculative purposes, in order to fill your head and store your mind with mere opinions, while you do not allow the book to influence your heart and life. That Bible is read best, which is practiced most.

## 7. Read the Bible Daily

Make it a part of every day's business to read and meditate on some portion of God's Word. Private means of grace are just as needful every day for our souls, as food and clothing are for our bodies. Yesterday's bread will not feed the laborer today, and today's bread will not feed the laborer tomorrow. Do as the Israelites did in the wilderness. Gather your manna fresh every morning. Choose your own seasons and hours. Do not scramble over and hurry your reading. Give your Bible the best, and not the worst part of your time. But whatever plan you pursue, let it be a rule of your life to visit the throne of grace and the Bible every day.

## 8. Read All of the Bible, and Read It in an Orderly Way

I fear there are many parts of the Word which some people never read at all. This is, to say at the least, a very presumptuous habit. *'All Scripture is profitable.'* To this habit may be traced that want of broad, well-proportioned views of truth, which is so common. Some people's Bible-reading is a system of perpetual dipping and picking. They do not seem to have an idea of regularly going through the whole book. This also is a great mistake. No doubt in times of sickness and affliction it is allowable to search out seasonable portions. But with this exception, I believe it is by far the best plan to begin the Old and New Testaments at the same time, – read each straight through to the end, and then begin again. This is a matter in which every one must be persuaded in his own mind. I can only say it has been my own plan for fifteen years, and I have never seen cause to alter it.

## 9. Read the Bible Fairly and Honestly

Determine to take everything in its plain, obvious meaning, and regard all forced interpretations with great suspicion. As a general rule, whatever a verse of the Bible seems to mean, it does mean. Cecil's rule is a very valuable one, – *'The right way of interpreting Scripture, is to take it as we find it, without any attempt to force it into any particular system.'* Well said Hooker, *'I hold it for a most infallible rule in the exposition of Scripture, that when a literal construction will stand, the furthest from the literal is commonly the worst.'*

## 10. Read the Bible with Christ Continually in View

The grand primary object of all Scripture is to testify of Jesus. Old Testament *ceremonies* are shadows of Christ. Old Testament *judges* and deliverers are types of Christ. Old Testament *history shows the world's need of Christ.* Old Testament prophecies are full of Christ's sufferings, and of Christ's glory yet to come. The first advent and the second, – the Lord's humiliation and the Lord's glorious kingdom, – the cross and the crown, shine forth everywhere in the Bible. Keep fast hold on this clue, if you would read the Bible aright.

# Appendix 3

## *Prayer of Saint John Chrysostom Before Reading or Listening to the Word of God*[1]

O Lord Jesus Christ, open Thou the eyes of my heart, that I may hear Thy word and understand and do Thy will, for I am a sojourner upon the earth. Hide not Thy commandments from me, but open mine eyes, that I may perceive the wonders of Thy law. Speak unto me the hidden and secret things of Thy wisdom. On Thee do I set my hope, O my God, that Thou shalt enlighten my mind and understanding with the light of Thy knowledge, not only to cherish those things which are written, but to do them; that in reading the lives and sayings of the saints I may not sin, but that such may serve for my restoration, enlightenment and sanctification, for the salvation of my soul, and the inheritance of life everlasting. For Thou art the enlightenment of those who lie in darkness, and from Thee cometh every good deed and every gift. Amen.

---

1. As found at https://cpress.orthodoxws.com/prayer_before_reading_scripture (Accessed January 25, 2021).

# Christian Focus Publications

Our mission statement –

STAYING FAITHFUL

In dependence upon God we seek to impact the world through literature faithful to His infallible Word, the Bible. Our aim is to ensure that the Lord Jesus Christ is presented as the only hope to obtain forgiveness of sin, live a useful life and look forward to heaven with Him.

Our books are published in four imprints:

### CHRISTIAN
## FOCUS

Popular works including biographies, commentaries, basic doctrine and Christian living.

### CHRISTIAN
## HERITAGE

Books representing some of the best material from the rich heritage of the church.

## MENTOR

Books written at a level suitable for Bible College and seminary students, pastors, and other serious readers. The imprint includes commentaries, doctrinal studies, examination of current issues and church history.

## CF4•K

Children's books for quality Bible teaching and for all age groups: Sunday school curriculum, puzzle and activity books; personal and family devotional titles, biographies and inspirational stories – because you are never too young to know Jesus!

Christian Focus Publications Ltd,
Geanies House, Fearn, Ross-shire,
IV20 1TW, Scotland, United Kingdom.
www.christianfocus.com